SCOBIE

A LIFETIME IN RACING

SCOBIE

A LIFETIME IN RACING

Scobie Breasley & Christopher Poole

QUEEN ANNE PRESS
MACDONALD & CO
LONDON & SYDNEY

A QUEEN ANNE PRESS BOOK

© A. E. Breasley/Christopher Poole & Associates

First published in Great Britain in 1984 by
Queen Anne Press, Macdonald & Co (Publishers) Ltd,
Maxwell House, 74 Worship Street,
London EC2A 2EN

A BPCC plc company

Typeset by Cylinder Typesetting Ltd, London

Reproduced, printed and bound in Great Britain by
Hazell, Watson & Viney Limited,
Member of the BPCC Group
Aylesbury, Bucks

This book is dedicated to May,
'my darling wife'.

Contents

Acknowledgements

May Breasley's praiseworthy hoarding instincts resulted in a rich source of both written and photographic material covering much of her husband's racing career. This proved invaluable as did Mrs Breasley's own notes and reminiscences. Valerie Burholt collated and edited these items and undertook considerable additional research. She also typed the text. Caroline North of Queen Anne Press somehow managed to produce a reasonably rational and cogent end product. To these people and to many others who offered help and advice freely and willingly, the authors owe a great deal.

Introduction

Arthur Edward Breasley, known throughout a professional racing career spanning more than half a century as 'Scobie' and properly renowned in both hemispheres, was one of the truly great jockeys of his era. He went on to train high-quality racehorses in England, France and the United States and, later still, to manage the string owned by Ravi Tikkoo.

But it is as a rider that this tiny, quiet Australian will always be remembered by those who saw him in action; the supreme master at keeping his mounts perfectly balanced and running straight. His concept of jockeyship was unique, his style inimitable and his skill legendary for all its utter lack of the flamboyant.

Yet controversy was an ever-present shadow across his great career in the saddle. Scobie's very arrival in England for the 1950 Flat racing season was prompted by a long and bitter dispute with a Stipendiary Steward in Melbourne who was convinced that Breasley was betting heavily and had become a 'bent' jockey. Suspensions for alleged rough riding were frequent to the extent that Breasley spent all but six weeks of one Australian season banned from competition. His entire career as a jockey seemed in jeopardy.

Those of us who became familiar with Scobie Breasley's ultra-passive style, his scant use of the whip and that unchanging and self-effacing smile in either victory or defeat, find accusations of rough-house tactics difficult to comprehend, but in these pages can be found his own explanation.

The Breasley race-riding philosophy, expressed with disarming frankness and simplicity, has made a fascinating study. Wisdom is not necessarily the prerogative of maturity but a professional of such vast and varied experience can be expected to have amassed great knowledge. Having spent many hours in conversation with Scobie and his wife May during the research period for this overdue book, I can vouch that this is the case.

Few people rode better than Scobie Breasley and few talk more lucidly or have more precise recall. Scobie was beleaguered by publishers and agents to sign contracts for a 'ghosted' autobiography or an 'approved' biography when he retired from riding 16 years ago. He turned them all away, certain that the moment was inappropriate. He felt that the gloss should be allowed to harden and the controversies fade before a proper perspective could be reached. Now he is able, with freedom and complete honesty, to look back across the wide and vivid canvas of a great international career. Breasley rode nearly 3,500 winners including a brace of Derbys, an Arc de Triomphe and no fewer than five Caulfield Cups in his native Australia.

Racing fans called him the Ice Man of Wagga Wagga in tribute to his imperturbable calm no matter how tight the finish or how valuable the race. Scobie rode precisely the same in a great Classic or a modest handicap; preferring to leave his challenge late and to be as easy as possible on his mount. A weighing-room contemporary coined an expression which encapsulates the Breasley method – 'Scobie would never win by a head if he could manage a short head'.

Yet, such was the perfection of his timing that very few races he should have won escaped him while a great number he was not really entitled to win were snatched by sheer impudence. Ron Hutchinson, a fellow Australian and a notable international jockey in his own right, claims that no-one could out-think or out-wait the Ice Man. 'So many times I would sit still and be determined that Scobie must make the first move', Hutchinson recalls. 'On some occasions we would be well inside the final furlong before my resolve cracked, but then the old fellow would come swooping down in the very last stride and I would know I had still gone too soon. The man was a genius'.

Scobie's championship battles with Lester Piggott enthralled a far wider audience than those sports fans who follow racing on a day-to-day basis, for they featured not only a direct confrontation between two supreme masters of their craft but, far more fascinating, a series of epic clashes in which an audacious and confident youngster met head-on a wily and wise veteran. It would be difficult to imagine two less similar men. Nor was there any great feeling of brotherhood between them although, true to say, each admired the other's professional skills and does to this day.

Scobie Breasley's assessment of his former rival and the comparison he makes between Piggott and such other great stars as Sir Gordon Richards and Rae Johnstone forms, I like to think, one of the most interesting and revealing sections of this book. Hearing one acknowledged expert discuss at length and in detail his opinions of equally talented professionals has been a rewarding and illuminating experience. Having been an admirer of Scobie Breasley for many years, I expected a high degree of expertise but the bonus of my subject's wit and humour came as a most pleasing surprise. Scobie is a great raconteur with a pungent and sometimes caustic line in anecdotes.

Having ridden from 1928 until 1968, a period widely claimed to have included the 'Golden Age' of between-the-wars racing, no-one could be better qualified to make comparisons between top horses and great riders than Scobie Breasley. But neither he nor I wanted to produce a book of boring and outdated reminiscences comprising a list of how horse A beat horse B in a race long-forgotten and probably of minimal impact in the first place – a format all too familiar in the field of sports biography.

Just as important as the story of an outstanding public figure is that of an unusual man. Scobie Breasley is not a candidate for sainthood – 'I've pulled the odd stroke, but then who hasn't?' – so an attempt has been made to produce an accurate portrait of a fallible but feeling character who, although now out of the intense public gaze he once tolerated with no little charm and understanding, remains a hero to many racing enthusiasts.

After all, 16 years have elapsed since Scobie Breasley put away his size-four riding boots for the last time, but mention of his name still evokes memories of high-quality race-riding and an individual skill unmatched today. The magic of Scobie appreciates rather than fades.

1
'I Believe in Santa Claus'

Scobie Breasley was a balding, 50-year-old grandfather when he rode the Irish-trained colt Santa Claus to victory in the 1964 Derby. To the impartial it was a predictable big-race success achieved with a typical final-furlong flourish, the hallmark of Breasley's jockeyship. But to the owners and trainer of Santa Claus the Derby result appeared unnecessarily and dangerously close – a snatching of glory when it could have been pocketed with ease.

Santa Claus had started favourite at 15-8 and was a popular winner but the congratulations which might have been showered on his jockey were, to say the least, muted. In fact, Scobie never rode Santa Claus again and now says still with a trace of bitterness: 'It must be a record – I'm the only jockey who was ever fired for winning the Derby'.

Quite apart from Scobie's natural inclination to come from behind on a horse known to possess top-class finishing pace, he had excellent reasons for riding the Derby favourite in a restrained style. Those reasons were fully endorsed by subsequent races but, unfortunately, the connections of Santa Claus never bothered to ask their jockey's opinion at the time.

'I always believed that Santa Claus would win the Derby because he had just the right combination of speed and stamina but he was not blessed with the soundest legs', Scobie says. 'He was a tall colt and I formed the view that he might not be suited any too well by Epsom. That's why I reached the decision that it was vital to balance him down Tattenham Hill even if it meant leaving us with a lot of ground to make up in the straight.

A smile that says 'I've won the Derby'. Scobie returns on Santa Claus after his 1964 Epsom triumph.

17

'In fact, he handled the track reasonably well for such a big, gawky horse but I was conscious, both before the race and during it, of keeping the risks to a minimum. He won easily, no matter how it looked from the stands. The owners seemed happy enough even if they didn't exactly swarm all over me. I suppose they thought I wasn't going to catch Indiana but I knew what was under me and always had things well in hand. If they wanted to win by 10 lengths but risk breaking the horse down they shouldn't have booked me to ride.

'Riding a race from the stand is very different from sitting astride a racehorse, particularly in the Derby. You try for 100 per cent concentration but at the back of your mind must be thoughts of all that prize-money and the even greater value of a Classic winner at stud.

'It must be even harder for present-day jockeys to keep cash out of their minds now that it's become fashionable to reward a big-race success by offering the rider a share in his mount when he becomes a stallion. Some of those guys must be seeing pound signs flashing at every stride, but in my day we were certain of nothing more than our straight percentage although, of course, we hoped for a present in cash or kind.

'I was trying to do a proper professional job on Santa Claus and still believe I did, but I was never asked to ride him again after Epsom. He won the Irish Sweeps Derby very easily, ridden by Billy Burke who had also partnered him to victory in the Curragh Guineas, but was beaten at Ascot when he started long odds-on for the King George and in the Arc when Jimmy Lindley had the ride.

'It may sound like sour grapes to say so, but if I had kept the mount I firmly believe Santa Claus would have gone through the remainder of his career undefeated. You needed to kid him a little. Not that he was ungenerous or at all kinky, but I'm convinced he used to feel those dodgy legs every now and then and went best when given a quiet and kind ride.

'As a matter of fact, I helped get Santa Claus beaten at Ascot. My old mate Bill Pyers rang to say Ernie Fellows was thinking of bringing a four-year-old called Nasram II over from Chantilly for the King George VI and Queen Elizabeth Stakes and as I'd

Rounding Tattenham Corner in the 1964 Derby. The winner, Santa Claus, is back in ninth place but perfectly balanced by Scobie.

ridden Santa Claus he wanted to know if they had a chance. Well, on the face of it, they didn't have a prayer but I told Bill that Santa Claus could be turned over if the going was firm and if they stretched him by setting a real gallop. It proved good advice.

'The Ascot ground was on the fast side and Bill set off in front to make sure Santa Claus knew he was in a race. I guess he was feeling those legs of his and that Burke was uncertain whether to go after Nasram or wait and hope the leader came back to him. In the end, he didn't really do either and Bill was able to keep a bit up his sleeve for the last furlong and hold on by a couple of lengths. Santa Claus started 13-2 on, one of the shortest-priced favourites I recall in a big race. His getting beaten was a real shock to most people but not to me. I'd have won on him that day but Billy Burke was inexperienced and, of course, didn't know about the great Australian plot.

'I suppose some people will think it a dirty trick but Santa Claus was no longer my ride and I was doing a favour for an old friend and fellow Aussie. Santa Claus was not the only King George hot-pot I managed to get beat but that's a story for later when I'm remembering the excitement of my many tussles with Lester Piggott.

'Jimmy Lindley, one of the top English riders of his day and a very decent bloke, picked up the ride on Santa Claus for Long-champ which didn't please me too much at the time, but he did nothing wrong in the Arc de Triomphe although beaten narrowly by Prince Royal II and Roger Poincelet. My Derby winner had missed the St Leger because trainer Mick Rogers considered the Doncaster going too firm after what had happened at Ascot.

'He only knew half the story! But Santa Claus looked right and was "expected" in Paris. He may have been a bit unlucky but I hope it doesn't sound big-headed to say I believe I would have won on him there, too. He was a horse who needed careful treatment. I knew him, Jimmy didn't – it was as simple as that. I rate Santa Claus a decent horse and the better of my two Derby winners. It's a pity we never got together again.'

Santa Claus, by Chamossaire, winner of a substitute St Leger at York in the final year of World War II, was out of the Arctic Prince mare Aunt Clara, the ninth foal of her dam, Sister Clara. The 1964 Derby winner was bred by a Dr Smorfitt, a Warwick-shire GP, who kept only one other mare at the time. The good doctor had brought the dam of Santa Claus as an unraced two-year-old at the Newmarket December Sales for the princely sum of 130 guineas. She ran only three times, without winning, and was then retired to the paddocks. Santa Claus was her third foal.

Santa Claus himself made only 800 guineas as a foal when offered in the same ring where his mother was bought so cheaply, but changed hands again as a yearling for 1,200 guineas to the bid of a British Bloodstock Agency representative, acting on behalf of Mrs Darby Rogers, mother of Mick Rogers, and Mr John Ismay, an enthusiastic owner of both Flat and jumping horses right up to his death in 1972 at the age of 87.

Naturally enough, Santa Claus went into training with Mick Rogers at Stepaside on the Curragh but did not come to hand early as a two-year-old. His racecourse debut was delayed until the August of 1963 when he started unbacked and finished unplaced in the six-furlong Anglesey Stakes – hardly an auspicious beginning.

However, just a month later he had made sufficient progress in his home work to earn a place in the field for the National Stakes, then Ireland's primary event for two-year-olds. The Royal Ascot winner Mesopotamia looked a moral certainty and started a short-priced favourite but Santa Claus, ridden by Billy Burke, won cantering by eight lengths.

Mick Rogers had worked something of a miracle in a few short weeks, and it was not only the Irish who were impressed with the acceleration Santa Claus displayed that Autumn day on the Curragh. Almost before he was back in his box at Stepaside, barely half a mile from the racecourse, Santa Claus had been installed winter favourite for the Derby.

A three-length victory in the Irish 2,000 Guineas the following May made Santa Claus the hottest property in European racing that spring, but after a council of war between the colt's owners it was decided that Scobie Breasley should be approached to ride at Epsom where, it was felt, Burke's inexperience would count against the favourite's prospects.

This was only sensible since the Epsom switchback is renowned throughout the international Turf community as the most difficult course in the world to master. The decision was also entirely in keeping with that taken by Mick Rogers in 1958 when he had engaged local specialist Charlie Smirke to partner Hard Ridden, with triumphant results.

In fact, Rogers had first considered offering Scobie the Derby ride on Santa Claus during the winter and approached him during his holiday in Barbados. Scobie had tentatively agreed, provided he was not needed by Sir Gordon Richards' stable, where he was retained. The invitation was renewed before the Irish 2,000 Guineas but Scobie was not free to take the mount in the Curragh Classic.

Santa Claus in the winners' circle at Epsom. Scobie was never to ride the Derby hero again.

'Gordon had nothing for the Derby and consented to release me', Scobie remembers. 'Naturally, I was delighted because Santa Claus was the form horse for Epsom and clearly had a great chance. Oddly enough, he was my 13th ride in the Derby so I've never been superstitious about that number since.'

Because Scobie was unable to make the trip to Ireland on Guineas day, his contact with Santa Claus was limited to a brief 'getting-to-know you' session on the gallops and since his services were so swiftly dispensed with after the Derby, he actually sat on the back of Santa Claus just twice. Yet, together they won what was, in 1964, the most valuable horse race ever staged in Great Britain. Santa Claus won a total of £134,387 during his short career, and despite those defeats at Ascot and Longchamp, was voted 'Horse of the Year'. A promising stallion career was cut short in 1970 when Santa Claus died following a thrombosis.

His major successes as a sire were Santa Tina, who won an Irish Guinness Oaks and further races in both France and the United States, Reindeer (Irish St Leger and Prix Kergorlay) and that conspicuously handsome colt Yaroslav, whom Sir Noel Murless trained to win Ascot's Royal Lodge Stakes.

Unhappily, Scobie Breasley's post-Derby sacking still rankles. 'I was promised a great deal but got nothing apart from my bare percentage. Funny way to treat a man who won a Derby', he says.

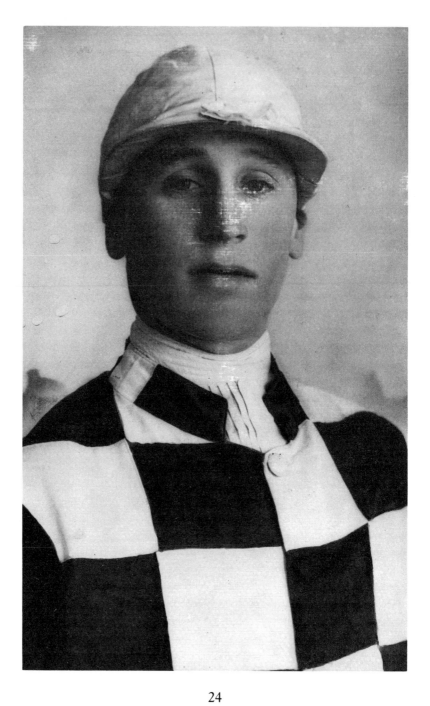

2

Scobie...the Naming of a Champion

Arthur Edward Breasley was born into the up-State farming community of Wagga Wagga, New South Wales on 7 May 1914, one of seven children of Sidney and Emily Breasley. His father was a horseman who combined sheep droving with small-scale racehorse training, saddling runners and trotters at the country meetings in the district.

Wagga, while not exactly a bush town, was distinctly rural in the first quarter of this century and horses, rather than cars, were still the most common means of both personal and commercial transport. The cliché so often applied to those who become professional jockeys, that they could ride as soon as they could walk, just happens to be true in Scobie Breasley's case.

It was natural enough. Not only did the young Scobie have the example of his father to follow, he also imitated his brother Sidney junior – known in the family as Bonny – who was eleven years his senior. Bonny Breasley himself was a jockey of considerable talent, riding in the Melbourne area both on the Flat and over jumps for many years. However, he had retired by 1950, the year Scobie crossed the world to try his luck in England and to become one of Europe's greatest race-riders.

Scobie loved the life of an Australian country boy and was never happier than on those occasions when his father took him along on a major sheep drive.

'It was great, if pretty basic. We would live under canvas, killing sheep for the pot and riding our ponies cross-country for many a mile. What lad could resist such a life-style? The sheep

Opposite: *The imperious look of youth. An early portrait of Scobie Breasley.*

we killed to eat served another purpose – we would dry the skins to sell. Wherever there was a major sheep sale in the area you would find the Breasleys. I enjoyed every minute and learned a lot, too. Droving gave me an appetite, but when I was at home in Wagga I rarely wanted to eat. It drove my mother to distraction and she was once reduced to bribery in an attempt to persuade me to eat. She offered me a shilling to eat a potato. It was a struggle, but I wanted that shilling.'

Despite Emily Breasley's efforts, Scobie never developed a normal desire for food. Even today he weighs hardly eight stones and eats little, but this lack of appetite was to prove a priceless asset during his long career in the saddle. The majority of jockeys need to practise an endless wasting regime in order to keep in check both their solid and fluid intake but Breasley has rarely suffered from this problem.

Perhaps surprisingly for one born and reared in a high-temperature climate, Scobie describes himself as 'a free sweater'. Heavy perspiration obviously helps keep body fluid levels low, and this is another natural attribute which saved him from a life-style ruled by semi-starvation and constant use of a sweat box or sauna. 'It doesn't seem to have much to do with either temperature or humidity levels', says Scobie. 'I still sweat freely even when it's chilly. If I had a ride late on the card I could always reckon on being a couple of pounds lighter by the fifth or sixth race than I was in the first. Lucky really.'

Lucky indeed when you consider the extraordinary lengths to which some jockeys go in order to keep below their normal body weights. Scobie Breasley is full of admiration for such men as Lester Piggott who, over a period of more than thirty years, has maintained his weight at some three stones under that which an adult of his height would normally scale.

'It must be a curse. Sometimes the temptation to have a right gorge must be almost overwhelming and I'm grateful that it was never really necessary for me to get involved in long bouts of wasting. But, naturally, my mother worried about me as a kid, not understanding that I really didn't need much food.'

Scobie Breasley was, you might say, born to be a jockey – equipped by nature with a powerful yet light frame, a keen eye and perfect sense of balance and brought up in an environment where riding was an aspect of everyday life. However, Emily Breasley was not very keen on the idea. Any enthusiasm she might have had most certainly evaporated when Scobie's brother was badly hurt in a racecourse fall. 'She didn't want another jockey in the family but never for a single moment did I consider making a living in any other way. I lived and breathed horses from as far back as I can remember.'

So the horse-mad youngster with little need for food but an unquenchable hunger for racing helped ride and look after his father's horses and ponies, learning all the time. He would get up on any horse he could find and because of this evident and all-consuming passion, Arthur Edward Breasley earned the nickname which has stayed with him for life.

'One of the biggest and best-known men in Australian racing at the time was the great trainer James Scobie of Ballarat. A friend of my father's, seeing how horse-crazy I was, said: "That lad of yours is a regular little Scobie". It just stuck and I've been Scobie Breasley for nearly 60 years now.'

Jim Scobie had a remarkable run of big-race successes in Australia during the early part of this century, saddling the winners of the Melbourne Cup in 1900, 1922, 1923 and 1927. When Clean Sweep gained the first of these triumphs in Australia's greatest race, Jim Scobie also was responsible for runner-up Malster, a feat achieved only once before when William Forrester saddled the first two to finish in 1897, and also once since, by the great modern-day trainer J. B. 'Bart' Cummings, who sent out Light Fingers and Ziema to be separated by only a short head in 1965.

Trainer Scobie's Melbourne Cup record stands comparison with that of Cummings, who achieved a hat-trick of victories in 1965-66-67 to follow that of his father Jim Cummings in 1950. But those successes were still many years into the future when Jim Scobie was setting Australian racing alight and building for himself a legend to stand alongside that of Etienne De Mestre, who trained no fewer than five Melbourne Cup winners in the space of 17 years, beginning in 1861.

Jim Scobie's overall record was equally impressive. For ex-

27

ample, during the 1900 season his horses dominated the scene by recording victories in the South Australian Derby, Victoria Derby and Australian Jockey Club Derby in addition to picking up the Moonee Valley Cup and the Williamstown Cup. Born in the Victorian settlement of Ararat in 1860, the great trainer was already elderly by the time young Breasley acquired his name but Breasley was still flattered by the association even though he might have preferred to have been dubbed 'Bobby' after his boyhood jockey hero, Bobby Lewis.

Lewis, also a Victorian and closely connected with the Scobie stable for much of his long riding career, won the 1902 running of the Melbourne Cup on 25-1 outsider The Victory, and was only a few days short of his 50th birthday when he recorded his fourth Cup win on Trivalve in 1927. Six of his Victoria Racing Club Derby successes came on horses trained by Jim Scobie and together they formed one of the greatest partnerships in the history of Australian racing.

Lewis enjoyed the reputation of being a friendly and likeable weighing-room companion but he was rather truculent on the subject of riding with short leathers, which was coming very much into vogue at that time. Jockeys who ride short, he was fond of saying, in no way improve their skills but do put their lives at unnecessary risk. The passage of years has not served to underline Bobby Lewis's views but he held them most sincerely, and undoubtedly he had the safety of his fellow jockeys at heart when he objected to what he considered a dangerous fad. 'He was the top man when I was a kid,' Scobie Breasley remembers, 'and I thought he was a tremendous rider'.

Despite his mother's reluctance to allow her second son to become a jockey like her first, Scobie's racing ambitions were being consolidated. By his 12th birthday, father Breasley – quite happy that Scobie should follow Bonny into racing – was making plans to get his younger son properly launched on a Turf career.

Following a short period as a stable-lad with Stanley Biggins, Scobie was signed up, at just 13 years of age, as an apprentice by the Melbourne trainer Pat Quinlan. The hopeful and enthusiastic youngster from up-country Wagga Wagga was, although he might not have realised it during those first few rather homesick weeks, on the verge of a fabulous international career.

Breasley had never been an enthusiastic scholar, but just how he came to leave his somewhat haphazard studies at Wagga State School two years early remains something of a mystery. 'I certainly didn't like school very much and quit in the sixth grade when I was 12. I seem to remember that Australian law required attendance until 14 but I managed to get out of it. I can't recall any trouble about my leaving early but in any case I don't suppose I was taking too much notice of the teachers – horses and becoming a jockey filled my thoughts and dreams.'

Yet, despite his lack of formal education, Scobie Breasley is an animated conversationalist once the barrier of his natural reserve has been breached, a man well able to conduct himself gracefully even in the higher levels of British social life. It can be said that he has now become the most distinguished Old Boy of Wagga State School, a gentleman at ease in all surroundings.

Scobie was once quoted by an Australian journalist as saying that he cannot recall ever reading a book. 'My education was gained after leaving school, I suppose. Travelling the world and meeting many influential people gives a man experience, and that cannot be acquired from books in the schoolroom.'

Even before leaving school, Scobie was riding at some of the up-country meetings in New South Wales. These semi-official fixtures were known as Picnic Meetings and were really nothing more than a Flat equivalent of point-to-points. However, his very first riding fees were gained at the circus.

When travelling shows visited the country towns in the district, schoolboy Scobie would compete – for a prize of half a crown – in contests to find the boy who could stay on a wild donkey the longest. The tiny lad from Wagga, amazingly strong in spite of rarely eating a square meal, was so successful that he was finally barred from competing, but not before he had pocketed quite a collection of silver!

Officially, Scobie Breasley's first recorded victory came at Werribee in 1928 when he rode a horse named Noogee to success in a handicap for three- and four-year-olds. It was his

29

19th ride but not a single member of the large Breasley family was there to share in his triumph.

'I still remember pretty well every detail of that race. I don't suppose any lad forgets his first winner or how he won. It wasn't much of a race but good old Noogee just got home in a driving finish and my career was underway.'

Just how many winners can be credited to Scobie? That must remain an open question. Not even the dedicated statistician Brian Hayes, who has tabulated with painstaking accuracy Breasley's riding records in both hemispheres, is able to provide a definitive figure.

The problem is that some of Scobie's early winners were obscure horses at equally obscure meetings. Consequently, Hayes' bound volume, presented to Scobie shortly after his retirement from the saddle, can offer nothing more definite than an 'estimated' total in Australia of 1,090 winners. In England he rode 2,161 which, together with wins in a handful of other countries, adds up to a career total of something approaching 3,500. 'That's a nice round figure, I'm happy to settle for that', Scobie says. 'I never kept records myself, always treating each day as it came. The next winner is what you need to concentrate on, not what happened yesterday, last week or last season.'

In any event, Breasley can be proud to have ridden more winners in Great Britain than any other overseas-born jockey in racing history. No wonder the little man from Wagga found a way to the hearts of British racegoers, an affection which still remains.

3

Apprentice Days...a Hard School

Scobie's early apprentice days were a curious mixture of public acclaim and official censure. An example came when he was just 16 and gained his first important success on Cragford in the 1930 Sydney Metropolitan. The youthful Scobie was elated, happy to have made his mark against senior rivals in one of the season's top races, when he was hauled before the Stewards. These gentlemen, an intimidating assembly for the inexperienced teenager to face, handed down their judgement that A. Breasley had crossed over to the rails too sharply. Although Cragford was allowed to keep the race, Scobie received a bawling-out and a two-month ban.

'It seemed hard to me', Scobie says with one of his wry smiles. 'But I was going to get used to kicking my heels. The Stewards were for ever on my neck and I picked up lots of suspensions – all of them for causing interference. I just loved those rails and would get against them no matter where my horse was drawn. Perhaps I was a bit brash but I think it was a question of "give a dog a bad name" and some of the Stewards were looking for me.

'It seemed that I was called in – and stood down – for the same things that other riders were doing and getting away with. When you're young and fearless you try tactics you would not attempt later in life, but you have to have a little devil in order to succeed. Perhaps some of the strokes I pulled did put other jockeys in danger but I don't think I was any worse than the rest.'

Scobie Breasley's constant brushes with the Australian Turf authorities were to be mirrored in England 30 years later by the experiences of his latter-day rival Lester Piggott, who found trouble on much the same scale during his own apprenticeship. The comparison serves to underline Scobie's point of view. The

Scobie gets Ocean Bound up to dead-heat with Finsbury in the 1930 Balaclava Stakes at Caulfield.

abiding will to win, when allied to youthful exuberance, can sometimes result in recklessness but officialdom should always take care that, in seeking to administer justice, it does not snuff out the flame of ambition. Fortunately, in neither the case of Breasley nor Piggott did this happen. Gradually, both these great jockeys learned to temper their desire for success with a measure of expediency, their careers prospered and, eventually, their paths crossed to the lasting benefit of the sport of horse racing.

'I was learning the hard way, sometimes suspended for longer periods than I was riding' Scobie says. 'Of course, I was still with horses in the yard but I'd enjoyed my first taste of the big time and don't pretend that I was not a little resentful.

'My boss, Pat Quinlan, was pretty understanding most of the time. But he was a funny chap, both hard and soft. He could make things rough on us lads one minute but be sentimental the

32

next. He had a quick and sometimes violent temper but he was always sorry afterwards – a hard man but a fair man. Pat taught me a lot about racing. He also taught me about betting. I've never been a big betting man and have always considered it a right mug's game but Quinlan liked to bet and sometimes put a little on for his riders. I guess I learned early that punters don't win in the long run.

'Some people in England thought of me as a betting jockey – no doubt some in Australia did, too – but they were wrong. I had a few pounds here and there but never seemed to ride well for my own money. Just the opposite in fact. If I had a small bet on another horse I would, like as not, get up and beat my own cash by a short head.

'Jockeys are, of course, strictly forbidden to bet but you would need to look a long way to find a rider who has never got a friend to put a few pounds on for him. Some jockeys are heavy gamblers but, I repeat, it's a mug's game. Just think about all the things that can go wrong. A horse can get left at the start; be interfered with in running or carried wide. No matter how good the horse is or how good the rider is, any number of things can go wrong during the course of a race. In other words, you can never be certain of getting a run for your money and that's why so many so-called "good things" get beaten.

'I always hated being asked for tips when I was riding and when I was training. As a jockey it's not a good idea to hand out information, even to close friends. Stable secrecy may be a bit overdone in some yards, but any rider should be expected to maintain a level of discretion. A blabbermouth is likely to find himself out of a job. When I was training myself, I still felt it was unwise to tell people when a horse was strongly fancied. If it was beaten you might lose a friend. It's just not worth it.'

Scobie, like all Australian apprentices, was taught to ride against the clock. Pat Quinlan would send him out to gallop a mile and a quarter in even time, in other words 15 seconds to the furlong. Or perhaps the trainer would order a three-quarter speed work-out at 17 seconds to the furlong. Such skills are not easily acquired but, once learned, become second nature and are never forgotten.

33

Few European trainers work by the stop-watch and, in fact, many disdain such methods as being at best mechanical and at worst pointless. Whether the European training system achieves better results than that used in Australia – and the United States – remains an open question, but what is absolutely certain is that stop-watch training introduces a wonderful sense of pace among the riders.

Breasley and his contemporaries who travelled the racing world were rightly renowned for their fine judgement, invariably avoiding the headlong charge in the early stages of long-distance events and frequently to be seen coming with a sweetly-timed late run to win from what might have seemed an impossible position a couple of furlongs from the finish.

'We boys would get a hell of a blowing-up or even a kick on the tail for being a couple of seconds off the pace either way when we were riding work', Scobie remembers. 'When that had happened a few times you learned the art, and after a few years you felt as though you had a stop-watch implant in the brain. In Australia it's taken for granted that a top jockey will have this skill, but in England not all riders, even those in the top flight, can judge the proper pace of a race with any frequency.

'Obviously, I think that riding work by the watch is the superior method but some English jockeys, notably Lester Piggott, are every bit as good at judging pace as any Australian or American. I think Lester was born a good jockey, just like Gordon Richards before him. Such great riders have an instinctive knowledge. They simply know when a race is being run too fast or too slow; when to kick on and when to keep behind. Lesser riders must be taught the tricks of the trade but the great jockeys seem able to teach themselves. I suppose it's a bit like playing the piano. You can have lessons to improve your technique but the basic skill needs to be there in the first place.'

Scobie Breasley clearly had that basic skill in very large measure and in Pat Quinlan a master well able to refine his natural talent. He soon became a successful and therefore fashionable apprentice, getting rides on fancied horses from outside his own stable. But the impish sense of fun and marked irreverence towards authority which has always been an element of Scobie's

34

character – still evident today and in many ways an admirable trait – often got him into trouble, both on and off the course.

Quinlan was private trainer to a wealthy businessman named J. P. Arthur who had extensive commercial interests in Japan during the 1920s. The stable-yard and accommodation for both the workforce and apprentices were located in the grounds of Arthur's palatial house in Melbourne. Scobie quickly recognised the difference in terms of luxury between his quarters and those of J. P. Arthur. What is more, he saw no good reason why the owner should not share – quite unofficially – some of his high standard of living with his employees.

Scobie has always been fastidious in the extreme and hit on the idea of using Mr Arthur's well-appointed bathroom when both he and trainer Quinlan were well out of the way. 'Our washing facilities were a bit primitive by comparison and I loved to take nice long baths so it seemed a good idea to make use of the boss's house. Another apprentice and I used to let ourselves into his bathroom regularly and emerge the best-scrubbed lads in Melbourne. Luckily for us, we were never caught or that might have been the end of our apprenticeship.'

Scobie is still liable to spend more time in the bathroom than in any other part of his house. 'I really don't know what he gets up to in there', his wife May says. 'Scobie baths and showers endlessly and is just as fussy about his clothes and shoes. He will happily spend a quarter of an hour cleaning just one pair of shoes and hates to be seen looking anything but immaculate.'

The resplendent Master Breasley created a degree of envy among some of his fellow apprentices and the other boys developed the habit of using Scobie's beautifully-kept clothes for their nights out – without asking his permission. Scobie countered this by buying a large padlock for his wardrobe in the lads' hostel but the others were not to be outdone and, when he was safely out of the way, unscrewed the back of the wardrobe and made off with Scobie's clothes anyway.

One day Scobie and another lad named Flemming decided to 'borrow' a motorcycle although neither had ever sat astride one before. With Scobie at the controls, all went well as they rode round and round but then came a major problem. 'I didn't know

35

how to stop it', says the man later to graduate to a Rolls Royce. 'The only answer was to keep riding until the bike ran out of petrol. That's what we did but it took an awful long time and we were worried that the owner might return before the juice ran out.'

Scobie's on-course scrapes tended to be of a more serious nature, with suspensions frequently interrupting his otherwise successfully budding career. Not that he was always the culprit – at this time Australian race-riding was a good deal tougher than would be tolerated today. Scobie recalls one particular brush with the senior jockey Bill Duncan, who badly and cynically interfered with the mount of his young rival when Breasley had a winning chance.

'I was furious, and the only thing in my mind as we returned to scale was to plant a punch on Duncan's nose, which, of course, would have got me into trouble yet again. Fortunately he defused the situation by saying "You'll need to catch me first – I'm a better runner, sonny." Sometimes things get pretty heated in the weighing-room but I've learned since that punching people on the nose is not the best answer.'

Brief reference has been made at the beginning of this chapter to Scobie Breasley's victory on Cragford in the 1930 Sydney Metropolitan – a landmark success for the future champion jockey of both Australia and Great Britain. But it should be remembered that both J. P. Arthur, Cragford's owner, and trainer Pat Quinlan needed to display courage and a high degree of loyalty to give Scobie, then an almost unknown apprentice, this ride in such an important and valuable event which attracted heavy betting. The Australian racing Press, even today far more opinionated and forthright than their equivalents in England, seemed unanimously against Breasley's booking. One well-known Sydney journalist went so far as to write an article questioning whether it was fair to punters that a big-race favourite should be ridden by an unproven apprentice.

But Arthur and Quinlan stuck to their guns, quite reasonably holding to the view that they were fully within their rights to allow 16-year-old Scobie to partner Cragford whatever the thoughts of the Sydney Press corps on the matter. Much of this

*The August Handicap at Flemington and an easy victory for apprentice
Scobie Breasley.*

argument passed over young Breasley's head, but there was a
good omen on the evening before the big race.

Scobie and his future brother-in-law, Bill Fisher, were
involved in a small-time poker school with several friends when
Scobie picked up four-of-a-kind. He decided to bet all he had –
actually 7/6d – and, needless to say, scooped the pot. Bill was
not exactly delighted at his future relative's good fortune but
Scobie himself remembers the incident with obvious relish. No
doubt he felt that his luck was in, and the win may well have
bolstered his confidence for the most important ride of his
career to date.

In any event, Cragford won the Sydney Metropolitan Cup
and Scobie Breasley, the unknown who should not even have
been trusted with the mount according to the local newspapermen, found himself a hero. He won another race on the
card but then came the crushing anti-climax of that two-month
suspension and Breasley returned to Melbourne with his
moment of glory sadly tarnished and facing eight long weeks of

working in the Quinlan yard without the prospect of another ride in public.

This pattern was to be repeated on numerous occasions with Breasley winning races of importance and high value only to fall foul of the Stewards and pick up another ban. But the successes were beginning to outweigh the suspensions and he was top boy rider in Melbourne for each of the last four years of his apprenticeship. Had it not been for his running feud with officialdom, Breasley's record would have been even more spectacular than it is.

Rising prestige sat comfortably on Scobie's shoulders. He has always been a modest professional grateful for the wealth and material comforts his career in racing has provided. Nor did he forget his family and the friends of his boyhood in Wagga Wagga. Even allowing for his wife's natural loyalty and respect, there is the ring of absolute truth about May Breasley's statement: 'I can honestly say I have never known or heard of a son who was better to his mother and father than Scobie. He treated them, the rest of his family and his friends wonderfully well'.

Pat Quinlan was obviously an important influence in shaping his apprentice's conduct and Scobie was also fortunate to obtain the friendship and advice of the barrister Eugene Gorman, who taught the young jockey how to look after and invest his earnings and to behave with dignity both on and off the racecourse. May says that Eugene Gorman is the one and only man her husband was ever afraid of but, far more importantly, he was also a man that Scobie came to respect and admire.

Gorman, himself a racehorse owner, was perhaps Scobie Breasley's severest critic. The following is an extract from a letter written to May Breasley many years after the event, in which he recalls the story of a horse named John Wilkes and the heavy betting losses he incurred because – as he saw it – of Breasley's over-confidence.

'In one of the races John Wilkes ran, Scobie sought to emulate a well-known Victorian rider named Billy Fulsham whose special line of country was to win by half a head. Pursuing these tactics, Scobie kept my horse tucked into a position where he need not have been with the result that he was unable to pull out and finished a not very glorious third instead of winning by a length or so.

'I had what was for me a very large wager. Certainly £400 or £500 which was, at the time, a matter of considerable moment. Not being desirous of being thought a bad loser, I merely sympathized with Scobie on his misfortune in running.

'The other incident concerned John Wilkes again and a horse named Charles Fox. I had raced the latter under a lease which had expired and within a week or so the two horses met in a race at Caulfield. It was a rainy day so I suggested to Scobie that he should put some resin on his palms lest he drop his whip . . . needless to say, he ignored my advice and Charles Fox beat John Wilkes by a head, Scobie finishing minus his whip.

'The financial consequences were again serious but I said nothing concerning the incident. Both these matters rankled, however, and on a third occasion when John Wilkes actually won, Scobie dropped his hands in the conventional fashion after John Wilkes had looked assured of victory only to find another horse flashing up and getting within a head or so of my runner.

'I felt that my opportunity had come. Scobie seemed rather pleased with himself but before he dismounted to weigh in I delivered myself of words which I do not remember exactly but the substance of which was: "You may think you are very clever. I have waited for today to tell you what I think of your riding. You have cost me two races about which I have made no complaint. Today I have won despite a tremendous effort on your part to cost me a third by dropping your hands when their was no occasion to do so. If you think this is clever, I . . . . don't".'

It is hardly surprising, then, that Scobie stood in awe of Eugene Gorman and little wonder, either, that he unquestioningly followed this gentleman's advice on business matters for years afterwards.

Eugene Gorman was Scobie's guiding light until the end of the Second World War, when he passed on the management of the jockey's financial affairs to Harry Ford, a man who became as much of a second father to Scobie as he was a business manager.

39

It was Harry Ford who first suggested that Breasley try his luck in England, an idea which was to have far-reaching consequences both for Scobie and for European horse racing.

4

Game, Set and Match!

The influences of Eugene Gorman and Harry Ford on Scobie Breasley's burgeoning career as a top jockey cannot be over-estimated, but in 1934 he was introduced to someone who was to make an even greater impression on him. This new acquaintance, forged casually beside the courts at a Melbourne tennis club, was with a young lady called May Fisher, the daughter of a local building contractor.

Scobie and May were introduced by May's brother, Bill, who sadly was not to survive the horrors of a Japanese POW camp in Burma. The two men had known one another for some while – Bill was present at the poker school on the night before Scobie's Sydney Metropolitan Cup triumph on Cragford – and the jockey was also acquainted with May's father, a keen racing man.

But May Fisher had no time for the Turf, ballroom dancing and tennis being her favoured leisure activities. Scobie was smitten but there seemed little prospect of romance since May Fisher was already engaged at the time of her first meeting with the jockey from Wagga Wagga. 'I never went racing and knew very little about Scobie, but I liked him straight away' May recalls. 'Scobie was 20 at the time and I a year younger.'

Scobie's pursuit of May Fisher, the belle of the Melbourne tennis courts, was every bit as determined as John McEnroe's quest for another Wimbledon title, although his courting strategy contained a deal more charm. 'I managed to see the other fellow off and May and I were married the following year', Scobie says. 'I'm not likely to forget the date, 5 November, 1935, for two very good reasons. Our wedding day was Melbourne Cup day and, even more significantly, the day on which Lester Piggott was born. He has no excuse for forgetting our wedding anniversary while May and I are always bound to remember Lester's birthday.'

Breasley's mount in the 1935 Melbourne Cup was the legendary Shadow King, a ten-year-old local favourite running in Australia's greatest race for the sixth and final time. He had finished sixth in 1929 and had subsequently twice been second and twice third. Scobie was promised a wedding present of £2,000 by Shadow King's owners if he could finally get the veteran home first and had also been guaranteed a further £1,500 by the holder of the Tattersalls Sweepstake ticket bearing Shadow King's name.

For the rather impecunious Scobie and his bride the possibility of landing cheques to the value of £3,500 represented a sizeable fortune at the time. 'I'm not sure whether I was more excited over riding Shadow King with all that cash at stake or about the fact that May and I were getting married the same evening', says Scobie with dubious gallantry.

'Shadow King and I had had a near miss in the Melbourne Cup two years earlier when we were beaten a head by the three-year-old Hall Mark after a very unlucky run. There were 18 starters that year – not a particularly big turn-out, but it was a very rough race and my mount seemed to get the worst of all the bunching.

'Jim Pike, one of the greatest jockeys I rode against in my early days, and who had won the Cup on the immortal Phar Lap in 1930, was the culprit. He brought his mount, Gaine Carrington, right round the outside of the field and then tried to cut in towards the rails. The rest of us were all left in a heap. There were plenty of hard-luck stories but none more genuine than mine.

'Hall Mark, winner of the Victoria Racing Club Derby and carrying only 7st 8lb, managed to miss all the trouble and go clear while I was still trying to get something like a decent run. When old Shadow King saw some daylight he simply flew and was catching Hall Mark hand over fist in the last half furlong. We would have won in just one more stride and you will still find people who were at Flemington that day to tell you that we did win.

'But, of course, there was no photo-finish in those days and the verdict went against us with the judge calling a dead-heat for third place between Gaine Carrington and Topical – the first dead-heat for a place in Melbourne Cup history.'

This was typical of the bad fortune which always haunted Scobie Breasley in the Melbourne Cup, a race he tried so hard to win but which was never destined to be added to his splendid record of achievements on the Australian Turf.

Nor was he any more successful in 1935 when so much money hinged on Shadow King's big-race performance. 'The old fellow did his best for me, but he was getting on in years by then and although he ran his usual good race, we could manage no better than fourth place behind Marabou who was less than half Shadow King's age. Incidentally, the winning purse for the 1935 Cup was £6,600 so you can judge just how much money £3,500 was nearly 50 years ago, especially to a guy who was heading for the altar a few hours after the race.'

Not that Shadow King's defeat was allowed to cast a shadow over the Breasleys' wedding in Caulfield that evening. May was resplendent in ivory satin and Scobie, always elegant, the very picture of sartorial perfection for the big occasion.

The Australian Turf authorities, sometimes considered every bit as autocratic and unbending as the British Jockey Club, made a heart-warming gesture in allowing old Shadow King and his bridegroom jockey to lead the Melbourne Cup parade although for them to do so was breaking with tradition since Shadow King wore number 7 on his saddle-cloth and was therefore out of sequence. Two previous Cup winners were in that year's field, Peter Pan and Scobie's old adversary Hall Mark, but Shadow King was held in special affection by the Flemington crowd.

'At least we were first in the parade even if we couldn't manage first place in the actual race', Scobie recalls. 'Of course, I was a bit disappointed by the result, but with something even more important to look forward to it didn't seem to matter all that much. Mind you, I won't pretend the money was not important; we were buying a house I couldn't really afford. In fact, to be honest, I couldn't even afford the £500 deposit, let alone the furnishings.

'Needless to say, when you need cash most urgently you can

43

never find any. Not only did I not win the Melbourne Cup but I couldn't win anything else, either. In fact, I didn't ride a winner for five months and, as any jockey will tell you, when the winners dry up so do the rides so I was going really bad, sometimes not being offered a mount for days on end, and those I was offered were no good.

'But then, luck always goes in cycles, particularly in racing, and out of the blue I had 11 winners in a fortnight. Everything was fine again and the cash was rolling in. May and I actually felt quite well off so I bought a car. Would you believe it, the very next day the Stewards stood me down for a month and we were back to square one.'

The newly-weds decided that since Scobie had earned an enforced holiday they might just as well use the 28-day ban to take a delayed honeymoon in Sydney. But more trouble was just around the corner.

Scobie and Pat Quinlan had a serious disagreement, the result of which was that Breasley's old boss refused to put him on any horse from his yard. Clearly, this split did Scobie no good at all. Not only was he losing the income and percentages from the Quinlan horses, but as news of their row spread – and nothing travels faster than bad news in the tightly-knit and slightly incestuous world of racing – he began to get the cold shoulder from other trainers who had been clamouring for his services only a few weeks before.

'It was a serious situation', says May Breasley. 'I was certainly very worried when we had a "roll call" of the family fortunes and found that, once we had paid the next instalment on our house, we would have had exactly £43 left in the world between us.' May, a lady who epitomises Australian straight talking, decided to take the bull by the horns, not to say the throat. She set off to confront Pat Quinlan in an attempt to end the dispute between trainer and jockey.

'Scobie was pretending to be unconcerned but I knew that he was just as worried as I was about this downturn in his career. We had also heard some very damaging things which Pat Quinlan was reputed to have said about Scobie, so it was obviously time to clear the air.

'As well as being worried I was also angry, but Pat soon put the record straight, telling me that the gossip he was credited with was just that – gossip. In fact, he made a point of saying that Scobie was the best horseman he had ever been associated with and that all we had heard on the grapevine was simply nasty talk put about by nasty people.

'I was very relieved. Scobie and Pat made it up and from that very day Scobie's career recovered. It was no time at all before our house was paid for in full and Scobie was soon riding well-fancied horses again and riding them brilliantly. I remember one particular race in Melbourne at about this time which I still think is the best example of Scobie's riding over all the years.

'He was up against Harold Badger, at that time the leading Melbourne jockey, and Titch Wilson in a three-horse race. Both were older and far more experienced riders partnering well-backed horses while Scobie was on the 33-1 outsider, named Elanage. Badger and Wilson went on early while Scobie waited . . . and waited . . . and waited. Just when it seemed the other two had it between them, Scobie pounced and Elanage stole the race. I never saw Scobie ride better and I know out of all his thousands of rides it is a race he remembers with pleasure, too.

'Like most of the jockeys' wives, I started going racing a lot and I can remember another rather special occasion of a very different sort when we were still struggling to make ends meet. There was a meeting at an up-country place called Yarra Glen at which Scobie had just one mount. His horse was no good and ran like it, but another jockey told Scobie that he was sure to win one of the races later on the card.

'Scobie's fee for an unplaced ride in those days was one pound, which he had collected. He gave me this single banknote and, pointing to a bookie showing 5-1 about the "good thing" that the other fellow was to ride, told me to stick the pound on it. He was watching from the edge of the ring while I went to place this huge commission but, having got there, I saw another bookmaker showing odds of 9-2. I knew so much about racing that I thought 9-2 was actually better than 5-1 so I had the bet with him. Scobie gave me such a telling off that I can't remember

45

whether we collected or not. It seems pretty trivial now but I felt very hard done by at the time, getting into trouble for trying to do my best.'

Lou Robertson was a trainer with whom Scobie Breasley was much associated at one time, and Robertson was a man who liked to bet and encouraged his jockeys by taking a little extra out of the ring on their behalf. Usually he would put Scobie in for the odds to a fiver or so on a fancied runner but one day at Caulfield, just as he was giving Scobie the leg up, he calmly announced that he had put his jockey in for £100.

'I nearly fell off again', Breasley says. 'When the horses lost I was expected to pay my share and I didn't fancy stumping up £100. Talk about a man inspired – I needed to be. Perhaps I was too concerned about the bookie's bill during the race. Anyway I managed to get the horse in a pocket; only just got out in time and won by a short head. That night we had a few friends round and one of them said to me "You looked a bit desperate today, I thought you were going to finish in front of the horse."

'I should think so!' Scobie remembers. 'He would have been looking desperate as well with 100 quid of his own money on. I reckon that race was the prime reason why I was never really a betting jockey. I found out that day that my nerves would never stand the strain! After all, £100 was a sizeable amount for a young jockey to have at risk by 1930s' values.'

Scobie's sense of humour is a well-developed facet of his character. It is evident only to those who know him well, however, as he is not given to obvious displays of any type of emotion. Consequently, casual acquaintances sometimes think he is taciturn, and newspapermen in both Britain and Australia have found the little jockey a difficult and reserved interviewee. Certainly he is not inclined to idle chat and, not unreasonably, seeks the assurance which only friendship or, at least, close contact over a period of time can provide before he becomes talkative.

But when Scobie takes you fully into his confidence an appreciation of both his wit and candour can soon be acquired. In this respect he is not unlike his great, former rival Lester Piggott. Both men keep their own counsel until such time as absolute

46

trust has been established. Then, however, the anecdotes come thick and fast. Few men can tell a racing narrative better than Scobie Breasley, who brings his jockey's eye for detail to every story. Among his favourites is the account of a singular race at Ascot – the Australian course rather than the setting of the Royal Meeting in Berkshire – which dates from the 1930s when, for once, Scobie managed to put one over those eagle-eyed Stewards with the help of his friend and rival Billy Elliott.

Elliott, the jockey who went on that ill-fated trip to America with Phar Lap in 1932, a journey which ended tragically with the death of the great New Zealand champion as the result of eating poison, suffered a unique brand of interference at the hands – quite literally – of Scobie that day at Ascot.

Both men were riding fancied horses and going head-to-head for the winning post when it dawned on Breasley that his opponent was getting just the better of the argument. Scobie decided to do something about this unhappy situation and what he did was to lean across and grab the unfortunate Elliott by the knee. Not only did he grab – he held on. The horses passed the post locked together and the judge settled for a dead-heat. Much upset, Billy Elliott lodged an objection but, fortunately for Scobie, without stating the precise nature of the alleged interference. To make a bold fist out of a tricky situation, Scobie lodged a counter-objection. The upshot was that both protests were overruled and the dead-heat ratified, to Scobie's delight and Billy Elliott's dismay.

Scobie would have been unlikely to get away with such a manoeuvre in modern times with the camera patrol video in operation, but Elliott, a kindly man who died at the early age of 35 as the result of diabetes, never gave the game away and the two jockeys became good friends.

5

Wartime and Billiards

Four years after the Breasley marriage, on 16 December 1939, May gave birth to a 5lb 9oz daughter in St Vincent's Hospital, Melbourne. Scobie was riding at Ascot that day, which proved to be a memorable one – and not just because of the advent of the little girl, who was subsequently named Loretta Janette.

A gang had planned to stage a massive fraud by cutting the telegraph wires linking Ascot racecourse with the relay station so that only a single broadcaster, an accomplice, could be heard on air. He was to delay the result of a particular race until after the placings were known, while other members of the conspiracy were placing bets off-course on a horse which had already won. It wan an ingenious if unscrupulous plot but, like a similar attempt at Bath racecourse in England nearly twenty years later, the scheme failed. The criminals missed cutting one line and news of the result of the Ascot race which, incidently, Scobie Breasley won, reached the outside world and wrecked the prospects of a big pay-off which would have cost bookmakers many thousands of pounds.

Scobie had another success on the Ascot card that day, but was left at the gate on a short-priced favourite after hearing the news of his daughter's birth. Perhaps his concentration lapsed for once . . .

Scobie proved to be a caring and affectionate father, lavishing virtually all his free time on the infant Loretta. 'He was even happy to change nappies', May Breasley says. But there was something of a family dispute over the baby's name. Scobie had won several races that season on a filly called Zonda and held

Opposite: *Scobie's wife May and their daughter Loretta smile for the camera of Melbourne photographer Allen Farrow.*

this horse in particular esteem. 'I know, let's call her Zonda', suggested the proud father in a flash of what he considered to be inspiration. May's response was some way short of enthusiastic. 'I'm not having my daughter named after some damn racehorse', she said.

The discussions, not always too friendly in nature, went on for several days with the name Loretta finally chosen more or less in desperation when Scobie came across a photograph of film star Loretta Young in a fan magazine. 'We both liked her anyway, and it's a pretty name so we finally settled on that.' But Scobie was to get his way over Zonda many years later when Loretta named one of her own daughters after Grandad's favourite filly!

By this time the world was at war. Scobie's riding opportunities became fewer although Australian racing was not restricted as severely as that in Britain and the rest of Europe. When conscription came to Australia to combat the encircling menace of Imperial Japan, Scobie failed his medical examination for call-up to the armed services. 'I thought I was very fit but the doctor turned me down because of an injury to my jaw which I collected in a fall some time previously. I can't pretend I was sorry. I doubt if soldiering would have been my game.'

Nevertheless, even a top professional sportsman, by this time a household name throughout Australia, was expected to do his bit towards the war effort. Scobie was instructed by the Emergency Manpower Commission to make himself available for work in addition to his career as a jockey. Scobie had a unique and varied series of appointments which included work in a local cheese factory owned by Messrs Kraft, helping to produce gas engines for cars as a way to conserve the scarce petrol resources, and becoming a nightwatchman on a wharf. He loathed all three jobs.

'The stink of that cheese is with me still', he claims. 'It was a truly dreadful smell which seemed to linger in your hair and on your clothes. Horrible. So was the engine plant because of the noise and dirt. The nightwatchman job, on the other hand, was too quiet. I used to go off with my little bundle of sandwiches knowing I wasn't likely to see anyone else until the next morning.

At least I hoped I wouldn't, because no one else was supposed to be there.'

The pressures of this enforced and utterly alien life-style on Breasley, essentially an outdoor man quite unused to the restrictions accepted by the vast majority of working men as normal, had an adverse effect on his married life. In 1941 Scobie and May Breasley separated to the surprise and distress of their friends and relatives.

Their parting was as civilized as that sort of thing can ever be with May and Loretta continuing to live in the family home and Scobie moving out. He is refreshingly direct about this unhappy phase of his life, dismissing it with a shrug and the words: 'I was naughty and got found out. The best thing seemed to be that I should leave'. But the separation was not to work. 'Scobie may have been able to stay away from me but there was no way he could stay away from Loretta', May Breasley remembers. 'In fact, he was in the house more often after we had separated than he was when he was living there. I remember thinking there wasn't much point in our being separated when, half the time, I walked in the front door and there was Scobie playing with Loretta. It was inevitable we would get back together. In the end, we did just that and made something worthwhile of our marriage.

'It was our good friend Eugene Gorman – later Sir Eugene – who brought about our reconciliation. Both Scobie and I will always remain in his debt and were delighted when he received his knighthood.'

Scobie, permanently back with his family, found a far more worthwhile method of helping to finance the Australian war effort. He had become a close friend of the remarkable Walter Lindrum MBE, surely the greatest billiards player the world has even seen. Lindrum held every conceivable world record for his sport including the amazing break of 100 in 46 seconds, set in Sydney in 1941.

Scobie himself was an amateur billiards player of well above average ability and he and Walter Lindrum hit on the idea of staging exhibition matches in various parts of the country, giving the proceeds from admission charges to the fighting

51

funds. 'We had a wonderful time and managed to raise quite a lot of cash as well' Scobie relates. 'Walter was an absolute master, one of the finest sportsmen I ever met. He was an untouchable world champion for years on end and I admired him tremendously. Our exhibition matches usually consisted of him playing and me watching, but even that was a pleasure.'

Walter Lindrum died in 1960 at the age of 61, but is still remembered by a worldwide legion of fans among whom Scobie considers himself privileged to be numbered. The great jockey, like most of his craft, has outstanding co-ordination and also plays a decent game of golf – an addiction which, some years later, was to play a vital part in restoring him to full fitness and so salvaging his career in the saddle.

Although the 1940s were a period during which Breasley achieved high levels of success – most notably in the Caulfield Cup – the war years left their mark on Australian racing. The Japanese attack on Pearl Harbour in December 1941 had brought the conflict unnervingly close to Australia's shores and two months later she became involved in the war at first hand when the Japanese Air Force attacked Darwin in the Northern Territory. Australia entered into a state of national concern with the Federal Government passing emergency legislation to conserve both manpower and materials.

Quite clearly, in these general conditions, it was not possible for racing to proceed in its normal form and the following September the programme was officially curtailed to permit the sport to continue on only three Saturdays in each calendar month.

Not even the Melbourne Cup was to be exempted from this regulation. Because of the emergency regulations, the Cup had to be switched from the traditional first Tuesday in November and, in 1942, was staged on Saturday, November 21 with reduced prize-money and the winning owner receiving a £200 'Austerity Bond' instead of the usual gold cup.

The Melbourne Cup attendance plummeted from more than 89,000 in 1941 to fewer than 36,000 that year with many of the crowd in uniform. Victory went to the 33-1 outsider Colonus with Scobie unplaced on Pandect, his now traditional ill-luck in

Australia's greatest race running true to form.

Scobie was still having problems with the Melbourne Stewards, too. During the 1942 season, already restricted by Australia's war footing, he picked up three major suspensions, one of twelve weeks, another of eight and a third lasting a month. These bans made for a very short year's racing and Scobie was becoming increasingly frustrated and angry at the official attitude to his riding which he considered to be competitive but fair.

'I actually considered giving up riding in Melbourne altogether – they had made sure it was hardly worth my while continuing in any case', Breasley says, still with a feeling of bitterness. 'I suppose it was about this time that I first started thinking about the possibility of riding in England once the war was over. I mentioned this to my business manager, Harry Ford, and while he did not rule out the possibility of going to England as a long-term plan, he advised me to seek an interview with Alan Bell, chairman of the Stipendiary Stewards, in the meantime to ask why I was getting such a rough deal from him and his colleagues.

'This was a very unusual request, perhaps even a unique one, and when I saw Mr Bell it soon became obvious what the real trouble was. He was convinced that I was a heavy-betting jockey. This was simply not true then or at any other time, but Alan Bell took a lot of convincing. In fact, I'm not sure even now that I ever did convince him but it clearly did no harm to put all my cards on the table. Mr Bell could produce no evidence of my alleged betting activities, simply telling me that he and some other Stewards had heard a lot of gossip. Looking back, I should have tackled him a great deal sooner but at least the situation improved after our meeting and my suspensions became far fewer. I don't recall being stood down again when I didn't deserve it.'

Breasley's meeting to clear the air with the chief 'Stipe' and the reconciliation with May heralded a far more settled period in his life, both professional and domestic. Scobie was able to see out the rest of the war without the threat of returning to either the cheese factory or the nightwatchman's hut and his career as a top jockey prospered.

However, the scheme to try his luck in Europe was never far below the surface although it was to be another seven years before Scobie both startled and horrified the Australian Turf community by packing his bags and booking a berth to make a fresh start in England at the age of 35, a time of life when most professional jockeys are contemplating retirement.

6

The Caulfield Cup King

Scobie Breasley's inability to win a Melbourne Cup remains the great regret of his notable career in world racing, but he did manage to land virtually every other important Australian event and to dominate the Caulfield Cup by recording successes on Tranquil Star (1942), Skipton (1943), Counsel (1944), St Fairy (1945) and Peshawar (1952), the latter during his brief return 'Down Under' following two years in England.

Although it is not my intention to fill this book with long lists of horse's names, this seems an appropriate point at which to record Scobie's unique tally of major-race winners in Australia and no apology should be needed for doing so. In addition to his remarkable stranglehold on the Caulfield Cup, he scored the following important wins which are grouped according to the States in which the races are run:

New South Wales A.J.C. Derby: Carbon Copy (1948).
A.J.C. Metropolitan: Cragford (1930).
A.J.C. St Leger: Gay Lad (1946),
  Carbon Copy (1949).
Sydney Cup: Carbon Copy (1949).

Queensland Brisbane Cup: Sanctus (1949).

South Australia Adelaide Coronation Cup: Donaster (1937).
Adelaide Cup: Donaster (1937),
  Sanctus (1948).
Adelaide R.C. Birthday Cup: Chatspa (1949).
Port Adelaide Cup: Sanctus (1949).

Tasmania Hobart Cup: Wingfire (1947).

Victoria	Caulfield Guineas: Kintore (1944), Royal Gem (1945), Phoibos (1948). Moonee Valley Cup: Orthelle's Star (1938), Haros (1943). Victoria Derby: San Martin (1944), Advocate (1952). V.R.C. Oaks: Three Wheeler (1943), Cherie Marie (1945), Chicquita (1949). V.R.C. St Leger: High Road (1942). Williamstown Cup: Shadow King (1933).

No wonder the name Breasley holds the status usually accorded only to stars of the cricket field in the little man's native land. An article in an Australian newspaper during the early 1960s posed the question 'Who is the best-known Australian in England? Donald Bradman, Robert Menzies, Joan Sutherland or Richie Benaud?' 'Leading the field by a long nose is Scobie Breasley' came the reply.

By this time Scobie had become an integral part of the British racing scene and every bit as popular in the Northern Hemisphere as he was back at home earlier in his career. 'Pommies' may be more restrained in both their adulation and criticism than the outgoing 'Aussies', but their affection for the veteran jockey from the other side of the world could not be mistaken. If not the best-known Australian name in the United Kingdom, he was certainly the most popular, despite Scobie's modest and self-effacing public image.

'I'm not really a public man', he admits. 'Some jockeys enjoy milking the racegoers' reaction when they have ridden a big winner but, quite frankly, I liked to get back in the weighing-room out of the public eye. I appreciate the racing public and enjoyed their support but I never did like being mobbed by crowds of well-wishers.'

Scobie had plenty of well-wishers when he rode Tranquil Star to a sweetly-timed victory in the 1942 Caulfield Cup, for this outstanding mare, owned in partnership by Richard Cobden and T. G. Jones and trained by Ron Cameron, was something of an institution in Australia during the wartime years. She ran in

56

more than 100 races, and carried off more prize-money than any mare in Australian racing. Trainer Cameron was of the opinion that no mare was the equal of his splendid chestnut at her peak over a mile and a half. Clearly, she was at her peak that day more than 40 years ago.

The Breasleys were still living apart when Scobie won this, the first of four successive Caulfield Cups. He was fortunate to obtain the ride on Tranquil Star in the first place. She was to have been partnered by an apprentice named Keith Smith but 48 hours before the big race Scobie's intended mount had a set-back, leaving him without a mount.

Jack Pierce, a friend of Scobie's, said that he could perhaps get him on Tranquil Star who had a first-rate chance of winning, but the senior jockey refused to even consider this move as it would mean 'stealing' the youngster's ride. Only when he was assured that Keith Smith would receive a full winning percentage should the mare land the big prize did Scobie consent to the switch.

Tranquil Star was badly drawn, No. 25 of the 27 Cup starters, but Breasley had her across to the rails within a furlong of leaving the gate. The leaders seemed to have left Scobie very little room to challenge in the home straight but he sat without moving and, just at the right moment, a gap appeared and he drove Tranquil Star through it to gain a stylish and effortless win. 'One of my better efforts', Scobie remembers with that famous smile.

This was Tranquil Star's greatest moment although she went on racing – and winning – until 1946. Unfortunately, she was not a success as a brood mare but Scobie, like most Australians, rates her as one of the best of her sex to have raced. 'She and the Sydney mare Flight, racing during the same period, were both top-class. And Tranquil Star was such a beauty to look at.'

The 1943 Caulfield Cup, at Flemington again rather than its traditional home course as a wartime expedience, was run in two divisions! That may seem difficult for modern-day racegoers to believe, but in order for the sport to be carried on in such adverse conditions it was necessary to make all kinds of changes. With too many runners declared for safety and with the authorities not willing to disappoint any of the owners prepared to start their horses, a divided race was the only practical answer.

Scobie rode Skipton, winner of the 1941 Melbourne Cup, to take one division at odds of 14-1, the other going to the Western Australian horse St Warden who set a Caulfield Cup record – and an unwelcome one for the majority of punters – by returning odds of 100-1. Some bookmakers, ever an inventive breed, offered a unique double on the two Caulfield Cup races and linked one division in doubles with the Melbourne Cup or both divisions in trebles with the Melbourne Cup. Although Dark Felt, the Melbourne Cup winner, started joint-favourite with Skipton (fifth) at odds of 7-2, it must be very doubtful that any backer managed to select either the treble or the Caulfield Cup double thanks to the 'no-hoper' St Warden taking one leg.

'It was all a bit of a muddle, really. But I was happy to have ridden two Caulfield Cup winners on the trot or, to be dead accurate, one and a half' says Scobie.

Counsel, runner-up at three lengths to Dark Felt in the 1943 Melbourne Cup, continued Scobie's extraordinary Caulfield Cup run the following year. A seven-year-old gelding, Counsel was a workmanlike rather than a star performer but by now Scobie was acquiring an invincible reputation in this particular race.

The Caulfield Cup was back in its rightful place in 1944, the course having been vacated by the Australian Army as the war in the Far East drew towards a close. Despite the shortages and restrictions still evident, Australian racing was in a high state of preparation for a return to full peacetime activities and by the following August the prohibition of racing on public holidays was abolished and the Melbourne Cup resumed its usual place on the calendar. The mare Rainbird won under Billy Cook with Scobie a well-beaten fourth riding joint-favourite St Fairy.

But St Fairy kept Scobie's great run in the Caulfield Cup going by winning in 1945. His run of four successive victories in Australia's second most important handicap remains a record, but Scobie needed some persuasion to take the mount on St Fairy, who was owned by O. R. Porter and trained by Theo Lewis. Owner, trainer and jockey were great friends but a decent horse called Lawrence was also entered for the Caulfield Cup, and Scobie was more enthusiastic about his chances than about St Fairy's.

Ossie Porter decided to apply a little pressure through May. He dropped the hint that if Scobie rode St Fairy and the horse won he would send Mrs Breasley a mink coat. 'Most Australian owners are generous in giving presents on top of the usual winning percentages but, clearly, this was an offer out of the ordinary', May recalls. 'But Mr Porter was unaware of two important points – I didn't like mink and, in any case, I had no influence whatsoever so far as Scobie's riding plans were concerned. When it came to selecting big-race mounts from several options, Scobie always made up his own mind and was very often right.'

As it happened, the Breasley judgement did not need to be exercised on this occasion as the connections of Lawrence decided to keep him in reserve for the Melbourne Cup, so Scobie took the mount on St Fairy to gain yet another Caulfield triumph. Not that St Fairy had an easy passage. Scobie, on the rails as usual, was very short of room on entering the straight but, fortunately, he saw daylight at the optimum moment, got his run and managed to beat the mare Rainbird, ridden by Ron Hutchinson, in a driving finish. This must have been a good-quality race since Rainbird went on to land the Melbourne Cup in commanding style, decisively reversing Caulfield form with St Fairy although it must be said that the latter failed to get a clear run at Flemington – Scobie's legendary Melbourne Cup luck doing the dirty on him once more.

May Breasley told the delighted Ossie Porter that if he still wanted to make good his offer of a fur coat she would actually prefer ermine. This most generous of owners not only sent May a magnificent ermine coat but also divided the Caulfield Cup stakes money between Scobie and trainer Theo Lewis. When Mr Porter retired St Fairy he presented this top-class handi-capper to the Racing Club to be used as the Clerk of the Course's hack. Scobie won races from six furlongs to a mile and a half on St Fairy and describes him as one of the gamest horses he ever rode.

The smile on the face of the tiger. Scobie Breasley, master jockey, pounces to win yet another race.

Seven years would pass before Scobie Breasley completed his unique nap-hand of Caulfield Cup victories. Two of those years had been spent in England, but at the conclusion of the 1951 European season Scobie and his family had headed back to Melbourne. The English experiment had not, apparently, been a total success and, if the truth be known, the Breasleys were homesick. It was intended to be a permanent return to Australia, a fact underlined by Scobie's purchase of a building plot for a new family house in the swish Melbourne suburb of Toorak.

In fact, as will be related, Scobie crossed the world once more in 1953, made England his home base and became the most

60

popular import from 'Down Under' since lamb chops.

But all of this was still unknown and even unpredicted when Scobie pulled on the black and white silks of Sir Sydney Snow and Mr A. C. Lewis as he prepared to ride the four-year-old Peshawar, 11-4 favourite for the 1952 Caulfield Cup. This was a sentimental moment for Breasley, since the colours were identical to those he had worn when Cragford launched him on the glory trail in the Sydney Metropolitan at Randwick 22 years earlier and Peshawar, like Cragford, was trained by Scobie's old mentor Pat Quinlan. When J. P. Arthur died his will directed that his colours should be handed on to Sir Sydney and Mr Lewis, already well-established partners in a small ownership syndicate which raced its horses in both Melbourne and Sydney.

'I remember thinking what a fairy story it would be if I could win my fifth Caulfield Cup for my old governor and wearing the J. P. Arthur colours which were so familiar to me as a lad', Scobie says. Unlike the majority of fairy tales in the hard commercial world of the Turf, this one had a gloriously happy ending when Peshawar, brought with a typical late Breasley flourish, beat the lightly-weighted King Amana by a length and a half to earn a prize of £10,000 and a magnificent gold cup valued at £400.

Scobie had only one uneasy moment during the entire race. This came soon after the start when the 24-strong Cup field was tightly bunched and Peshawar clipped the heels of another runner. He stumbled and his head nodded. But he soon recovered, and with two furlongs left to cover Scobie had the favourite ideally placed in fifth position, just a couple lengths off the pace. A furlong later, Breasley knew the race was won but his now celebrated habit of doing no more than necessary made the finish look rather more dramatic than it really was. Only in the last 50 yards did Scobie allow Peshawar to forge clear, giving his mount an inch or two of rein and merely waving the whip to keep the winner up to his work.

Caulfield was ecstatic. One of her favourite sons had returned in triumph. Scobie and Peshawar enjoyed an enthusiastic reception with the cheers swelling again as Mr Lewis, flanked by Breasley and Pat Quinlan, stepped forward to receive the Cup from Sir William McKell, the Governor-General.

61

Scobie's ability to pick up major races with great regularity was still a feature of his riding when he returned to Australia. During the 1952 season he won another Victoria Derby riding Advocate, the Bagot Handicap on Prince O' Fairies and the Goodwood Handicap on Jamboree, in addition to the Caulfield Cup. But his Melbourne Cup luck failed to improve when Peshawar finished out of the money behind 5-1 favourite Dalray, ridden by the stylish Bill Williamson, another Australian destined to add a further dimension to his career by riding in Europe.

In all, Scobie made 16 attempts to ride a Melbourne Cup winner, starting in 1929 when Nightmarch scored from Paquito with the mighty Phar Lap, the even money favourite, only third. Phar Lap carried 9st 12lbs to victory the following year. Scobie's 1929 mount, Taisho, finished unplaced at odds of 20-1 and carried only 6st 11lbs. Four years later Breasley came closest to success when beaten by a head on Shadow King. In 1946 he again partnered a runner-up in On Target but this time was defeated five lengths by Russia, ridden by Darby Munro, whose niece Noelene is married to the former leading British jockey Geoff Lewis, now a successful trainer at Epsom.

Scobie gained another Melbourne Cup place on Ortelle's Star in 1938, but this third-placed mount was also well beaten. He finished fourth in 1935 (Shadow King) and 1945 (St Fairy) and was unplaced on the other 11 occasions. 'I tried my absolute best for what seemed year after year but it was just not on the cards for me to win a Melbourne Cup' is Scobie's postscript.

7

The Aussie Druid

It was in 1947 that Scobie Breasley began to think more deeply about his long-held but somewhat vague ambition to ride in England. He was greatly encouraged by business manager Harry Ford who held the view that his client could go on for years being leading jockey in Australia without making any great impact on world racing. 'If you want to be a really great rider the only place to establish your reputation is in England', Ford told him on many occasions.

Scobie was enthusiastic about the idea which is more than can be said of May. But it is a major undertaking, and one demanding no little courage, to uproot a career from one country and attempt to transplant it to another. Racing fashions can be fickle and Scobie had to face the possibility that he might not catch on in England while, at the same time, lose his popularity with owners and trainers at home.

'I was taking a big risk, no doubt about that', says Scobie with due reflection. 'But Harry Ford was right and I really wanted to spread my wings. I wasn't getting any younger, so if I was going to make the move it had to be within a couple of years or so. Harry Ford finally made a trip to England during 1949 and I asked him to try and get me a decent job there.

'As it happened, he came back with two offers of retainers for the 1950 English season but had been most impressed by meeting the flour millionaire J. V. Rank and recommended I take up the position of stable jockey to his trainer, Noel Cannon, at the Druid's Lodge Stable on Salisbury Plain. Needless to say, I hadn't any real idea where Salisbury Plain was but Ford knew that Mr Rank and Noel Cannon had a good set-up and sold me the idea.'

The marathon move from Melbourne to Stonehenge – that mysterious circle of gigantic stones around which the Druids worship the sun on Midsummer day – was on. If Scobie and May had their doubts about the wisdom of travelling halfway round the world to try their luck in England, they managed, for the most part, not to let them show.

Australian racing circles reacted to Scobie's impending departure at first with disbelief and subsequently with disappointment, but his fellow professionals determined to give the Melbourne champion a send-off to remember. Melbourne's Hotel Australia was chosen as the venue for a dinner in Scobie's tribute which was held on 9 January 1950, the organizing committee reading like a massive extract from the Who's Who of Australian racing and with the Lord Mayor of Melbourne, Councillor the Honorable James S. Disney, in attendance.

More than 200 people sat down to dine on Oysters American, Toheroa Soup, Schnapper Caprice, Roast Duckling with Orange Salad, Bombe Alaska and coffee – just the sort of meal to send Scobie on his way about half a stone overweight! No mention of alcoholic refreshment appears on the menu for this sparkling social occasion, but no doubt the guest of honour – no drinking man by his own admission – felt obliged to respond to all those toasts to his future success.

Scobie was also presented with a more tangible memento, a large and impressive volume bound in leather and inlaid with gold leaf, summarizing in both words and photographs his riding career from his apprentice days until 1949. This labour of love was undertaken by an expert calligrapher named James S. Forman, superbly lettered on parchment and signed by each and every guest at the dinner. Very properly, it remains one of Scobie's most treasured possessions.

'I was flattered. It takes something like that for anyone to realise how many friends they have. But it made the actual leaving all the harder. Australia and England seemed a lot further apart in those days and we, like the majority of travellers between the two countries, made the journey by boat via Bombay. That gave plenty of time to think about whether we had made a mistake even though it was, of course, too late to turn the ship round.'

The Breasleys had never before left Australia but soon became

64

caught up in the agreeable life-style of international tourism and went ashore to sample the colourful delights of Bombay, that great city which earned its nickname of The Gateway to India during the days of the Raj. After a long and exhausting day of sightseeing, Scobie and May returned to their ship to be told their were visitors to seem them in the Captain's stateroom. Puzzled, they made their way to the Captain's quarters to find the English jockey Bill Rickaby and his wife Bridget, who had called to wish the travellers bon voyage on the second leg of their long trip and to wish Scobie good luck in England.

'Bill was spending the winter riding in India and, having heard on the jockeys' grapevine that I was in town, had actually taken the time and trouble to pay a visit although we had never met before. May and I thought it was a wonderful gesture of friendship and, we discovered later, an example of the comradeship to be found in racing throughout the world. Somehow, we felt less homesick at once.'

Bill Rickaby came from a famous racing family. He was born in 1917, just a year before his father, Frederick Lester Rickaby who was also a highly-successful jockey, was killed in action while serving in France with the Royal Tank Corps. Frederick Lester Rickaby's sister, Iris, married Keith Piggott and named her son in memory of the brother who failed to return from the Great War, killed at the early age of 24. Scobie and Bill Rickaby were to ride against each other on many occasions in England and in the 1,000 Guineas of 1961 Breasley finished third to Rickaby and Sweet Solera when partnering Indian Melody. As for Rickaby's cousin Lester Piggott, he was, of course, to be Scobie's greatest rival during the Australian's highly-successful career in the Northern Hemisphere.

Bill Rickaby himself went on riding until 1968, retiring from the saddle at the same time as Scobie. He then took a post as an assistant Stipendiary Steward to the Royal Hong Kong Jockey Club but not long after arriving in the Far East was gravely injured in a car crash and obliged to return to England to live quietly at Newmarket. Bridget Rickaby is the sister of former Newmarket trainer Ryan Jarvis, whose son Willie was, many years later, to spend some time in Australia as pupil to Scobie's friend George Hanlon, the Melbourne trainer. Willie Jarvis is currently assistant to the leading Newmarket trainer Henry Cecil following another spell 'Down Under' with Tommy Smith in Sydney.

Such cross-references serve to illustrate how intimate and inter-linked the world of international racing has become with the ease of air travel but it should not be forgotten that more than 30 years ago when Scobie and May Breasley disembarked from their liner at Southampton they were engaged on a major adventure, walking a path that few had trodden before. 'We were, it seemed, a million miles from home', May recalls. 'Nothing was familiar and the weather was bitterly cold. But we had taken the plunge and Scobie was determined to show the world what he could do.'

Noel Cannon had been training at Druid's Lodge, a remote but beautiful yard about halfway between Salisbury and Stonehenge, since 1935 following a spell at Bedford Cottage, Newmarket. A highly competent horsemaster who placed his runners with care and foresight, Cannon was soon winning major races for Mr Rank. The 1938 season was one of almost unbroken success during which Cannon saddled Scottish Union to win the St Leger in the Rank colours, that colt having run second in both the 2,000 Guineas and the Derby.

The top-class stayer Epigram carried off Ascot's Queen Alexandra Stakes, the Goodwood Cup and the Doncaster Cup while Black Speck won both the Newbury Summer Cup and the Liverpool Autumn Cup for Druid's Lodge. At the season's end, J. V. Rank was runner-up in the list of winning owners. Cannon also sent out Why Hurry to win the wartime substitute Oaks of 1943 and, just the year before Scobie Breasley's appointment as stable jockey, provided seven winners – six of them in successive races – at the Salisbury August fixture. Noel Cannon liked nothing better than to produce a string of winners for his friends to back at his local course and was, quite understandably, popular in the district with all but the bookmakers.

So it was into this well-established, well-run stable that Scobie eased his way during the chilly early spring of 1950, far from home and surrounded by the unfamiliar but made to feel wel-

66

come from the outset. His partnership with Rank and Cannon was to have a highly auspicious beginning.

'It would be difficult to think of anywhere more unlike Melbourne,' Scobie says. 'But Druid's Lodge was a wonderful place to train horses. The gallops were magnificent and so varied, and we had all that space, all that wonderful old Downland turf, to ourselves. Mr Rank had arranged a cottage for us to live in, very comfortable and pleasant, and both May and Loretta liked to drive into Salisbury to shop. Of course, the English climate was a bit of a shock. You can't really prepare yourselves for English weather . . . you just pile on extra clothes and hope that you'll get used to it in due course. You never do.'

There was no outstanding prospect in the stable for the 1950 season, but Scobie found a decent crop of horses at Druid's Lodge and, as the weeks of preparation wore on, the gradual warmth which suggested that summer was on the way spread across verdant Salisbury Plain, and an English trainer built up respect and understanding with his new Australian jockey. Breasley began to relish the prospect of the new season ahead.

It was typical of Noel Cannon to try and give his jockey a flying start in England, and he decided to take Promotion and Decorum, two of the most forward members of his string, to Liverpool for Scobie to ride in the Ocean Plate and Molyneux Cup respectively.

Aintree racecourse at Liverpool, home of the Grand National, that most famous and most fearsome of steeplechases, is now used exclusively for jump racing but in those days the opening fixture of the season there was a mixed affair, the weighing-room a babble of banter between the Flat jockeys and their National Hunt colleagues. Into this tightly-woven and rather exclusive environment with its decidedly clubby atmosphere came the little man from Wagga Wagga.

He must have felt about as far out of his element as a goldfish in the Atlantic Ocean. Nor was the Aintree track itself in any way familiar with its vast expanse of 'chase, hurdle and Flat courses set down in unlovely urban Merseyside. A sombre, foggy place, it had nothing but the horses to remind Scobie of the sunshine and glamour he associated with racing back at

Flemington or Caulfield. But although the chill surroundings affected his nerves, Scobie did not allow this to show and certainly had no intention of letting it disturb his riding. Both Promotion and Decorum, his first two rides outside Australia, won and Breasley enjoyed instant acclaim from the British racing Press and public.

'What a start! I could hardly take it in, but when I did it was a great feeling. Suddenly Liverpool seemed to be the most lovely place on earth. I'm not normally very emotional but this was a special feeling and I don't mind admitting that I returned to scale with tears in my eyes.

'Of course, I owed it all to Noel Cannon who had been so determined to get me off to a good start. Noel thought that Promotion might not be quite good enough to win but he did fancy Decorum quite strongly. For them both to go by was a dream and gave me great confidence. So I came away from Liverpool with a 100 per cent record – two rides and two winners – also having fixed up a second retainer to partner the horses owned by Sir Malcolm McAlpine and trained by Vic Smyth. I felt as though I had won the Derby and Melbourne Cup rolled into one. For an Australian, almost unknown in Europe, to arrive and beat the English jockeys in his first two races was better than either May or I had dared to hope.

'Too good to last, of course, but I soon won another race – at Windsor – on a horse of Sir Malcolm's called Rose Lightning, and was beginning to find my feet and get to know the way round. I had also made a very special friend in Gordon Richards. He was the great champion, unchallenged and brilliant – the very best jockey I ever rode against or even saw ride. Yet he went out of his way to make a stranger feel at home. If I had doubts about anything I knew I could ask Gordon and, what's more, I soon came to value his opinions. Not just about racing, either. He was, and has always remained, so down to earth and straightforward. A great sportsman and a man of great common sense.'

The friendship of these two fine jockeys who had learned their craft at opposite ends of the world remains as firm today as it was back in the early 1950s. And the respect is mutual.

'Scobie is a great character and he was a superb rider,' says Sir Gordon. 'His horsemanship was equal to anyone's and when I retired from riding and began to train it never even crossed my mind to want another man as my stable jockey. He began riding for me in 1956 and we were partners right up until the time that Scobie himself gave up, 12 years later. We didn't always agree about everything – no two people do I suppose – but we hardly ever got to the point of arguing. It was a very happy and successful partnership.'

The friendship, support and, ultimately, the patronage of Gordon Richards should not be underestimated in discussing Scobie Breasley's highly-successful riding career in England. Richards, the man some wit dubbed England's shortest knight when he received the accolade from the Queen in 1953, is a man of high influence in Turf circles, perhaps all the more so because he has never quite appreciated his own fame and remains modest and easy-going in spite of the acclaim of both his peers and the racing public. 'For Gordon to take a liking to me made all the difference when I first got to England', admits Scobie. 'Real friends are never easy to find and he proved one of the best.'

The two men's wives also became close with Margery Richards helping May Breasley become acclimatized to English-style living and shopping. All four would often travel to race meetings together and later even took holidays in each other's company. No-one outside the Richards family mourned more when Lady Margery died than the Breasleys.

But, despite the help and advice Gordon Richards gave to Scobie on his arrival in England, the Australian jockey was strictly on his own once the starting tapes were released. 'You got no favours from Gordon in a race, he was a hard little bugger', recalls Scobie with some feeling.

Race-riding is, in any case, a solitary trade. No matter how carefully an event may have been planned, no matter how well-trained the horse in question, once the race is underway a jockey must always be alert enough, brave enough and clever enough to alter tactics in a split second. This is, essentially, the difference between competitive riding and riding for simple pleasure. Scobie, he of the almost uncanny anticipation, ice-

cold nerve and perfect timing, found it necessary to go through a period of re-training when he began the new chapter of his career in England. He was utterly familiar with Australian courses and Australian conditions. But this was a whole new ball game.

'I found I had a lot to learn. The variety of British racecourses is huge. Just think of the difference between Newmarket, with all that wide, open space, and a little circuit like Chester, on the turn all the way. Your tracks go left-handed and right-handed, uphill and downhill, some are vast and some are tiny; some straightforward and easy, others tricky and difficult. And a jockey, at least anyone hoping to be a top-class jockey, needs to get to know them all well. It's not easy, but having so many courses does take the boredom out of English racing. It also means a lot of driving about the country and it took me a little while to find my way round the roads, let alone the tracks!'

But Scobie learned fast. And the winners started to flow. Investigate and Idealist won at Salisbury to give him a first English double. Back on the old-established Wiltshire track in the July of 1950 he recorded his first treble since leaving Australia and picked up a further four winners at the three-day fixture. The Royal Hunt Cup, the biggest-betting race of the Royal Ascot meeting, fell to Scobie on Mr Rank's horse Hyperbole and a first visit to glorious Goodwood, the Sussex course that Englishmen claim to be the most beautiful in the world, brought another big-race triumph on Strathspey in the Goodwood Stakes.

Already his decision to quit Australia was paying dividends and already English owners, trainers and his fellow jockeys were appreciating that a rider of unusual skills had come among them. But racing is a fickle mistress and trouble was just around the next bend.

That bend, to be exact, is located on the downhill sweep towards the finishing straight at Brighton, the seaside track which attracts crowds of racegoers on holiday at this celebrated resort. Scobie, riding his old friend Rose Lightning, took a

Opposite: *Conversation piece. Scobie chatting with Sir Gordon Richards –* '*the greatest jockey I ever saw*'.

heavy fall when his mount slipped and shot him from the saddle. It put him out of action for three weeks at a busy stage of the season.

Scobie was running into trouble in other directions, too. He found Pat Rank, the heavy-betting wife of his patron, a difficult woman to tolerate. She had a high-handed manner and clearly looked upon jockeys – even those of Scobie's eminence – as little superior to servants. Scobie did not like her. He makes no bones of saying so now and, more importantly, let his feelings show at the time. 'If I'm polite to people I expect them to be polite back, whoever they are', he says with sound logic. 'Mrs Rank seemed to think that treating jockeys like human beings was below her dignity. I let her know she was wrong, at least in my case, and she didn't like it very much.'

But there was an even darker cloud on the horizon. A handful of professional Australian punters hit town with the intention of making a quick killing if they could talk Scobie into divulging stable information. The Aussie Ring, as these doubtful visitors became known, came close to doing Scobie's reputation great harm but, fortunately, he saw the danger in time. 'This was where I came in', he says. 'And I was not going to be accused of being a crooked jockey again.' But, in effect, that is just what did happen . . .

8

Classic Success...and a Change of Mind

Scobie Breasley began to receive telephone calls from a few people whom he had known casually back in Australia. Little chats between ex-patriots were natural enough and, so far as the jockey was concerned, perfectly harmless. One caller in particular started asking which of Scobie's mounts had a chance. Scobie saw no point in not telling him since the Druid's Lodge stable was run on very open lines and the majority of the horses in question had public form, there for all to see on the racecourse or easily gleaned by glancing in the newspapers or delving in the form book.

'This character told me he was over on holiday from Sydney', Scobie remembers. 'In those days you could only take £750 out of the country and it never really crossed my mind that he could be a big betting man for that reason alone. I couldn't see how he would have enough cash to make much impact on the betting market.

'Then he came up to me at Sandown Park one day to ask about the chance of a horse I was riding for Vic Smyth. I said it would run pretty well but that, in my view, it was not quite good enough to win. He went off quite happy so far as I could see and the horse ran into a place after I had given it every chance. That was the end of the matter as far as I was concerned.

'I couldn't have been more wrong, because later that same afternoon I was told that the horse in question had opened favourite and then taken a walk in the market. In other words my so-called mate from Sydney was not backing horses he was laying them or, at least, passing on the word to some English bookmaking friends of his to do so. No wonder he seemed happy when I told him the horse wasn't good enough to win. He wasn't looking for winners at all, what he wanted to find out about was likely losers.

'To say I was furious would be an understatement. I was absolutely livid. This man and a few other cronies were putting my entire career in jeopardy. There was only one thing to do – go straight to Mr Rank and tell him what had happened before someone else did or, even worse, reported the matter to the Jockey Club. I had been caught – taken for a ride – and I just had to put things right. J. V. Rank undersood the situation at once and told me that he fully accepted my version of what had been going on. But the Windsor affair cost me my retainer with Sir Malcolm McAlpine.

'Needless to say, when I saw that character from Sydney again I told him exactly what I thought of him and his methods of doing business. He cleared off as fast as his legs would carry him and I was mighty glad to see him go. But the whole thing left a very nasty taste in the mouth and made me feel very nervous about talking to anyone I didn't know well and didn't know to be trustworthy.

'Of course, I know about all the talk that went on. To hear some people on the subject, all jockeys are crooks and Australian jockeys are super-crooks. But most of what was said is total nonsense and the facts about the Aussie Ring, so far as I was concerned, are just as I have stated here. Racing is always full of rumour; it seems to thrive on it. But I never did anything at any stage of my riding career of which I am ashamed. I was never what could be called a betting jockey and I was never in the pocket of any bookmaker. And that's the simple truth.'

As Scobie's first season in England wore on the atmosphere between him and Mrs Rank became even more frigid. Pat Rank did not keep her own horses with those of her husband at Druid's Lodge and had no claim on Breasley's services as a jockey, but one day she as good as ordered him to ride a runner of hers at Birmingham. Scobie was not down to attend at the Midlands track that day and refused to take the ride. 'But I want you to go there, Breasley. You must go', retorted Mrs Rank in her most dictatorial style. Scobie dug his heels in and once again refused.

'That woman really got my back up. Breasley do this and Breasley do that without ever a please or thank you. I wasn't

74

having her talk to me like that and I had no plans to travel up to Birmingham to ride her horse. But then J. V., a real gentleman, came to see me and said: "I would deem it a great favour, Scobie, if you would agree to ride my wife's horse for her." Well, that was different so I agreed. I'm not sure what happened at Birmingham but I think the horse was beaten!'

Mrs Rank was a fearless backer. As far back as 1938 she had had £10,000 on a two-year-old at Royal Ascot – a winner – and she shared with another lady owner, the Hon Dorothy Paget, the doubtful honour of being considered the biggest punter in English racing between the wars and for some time afterwards.

Geoffrey Hamlyn, for many years the senior starting price reporter on the *Sporting Life* and England's most authoritative expert on horse race betting, can recall and document many examples of wagers struck by both women which would curl the hair of modern-day bookmakers. 'Both Mrs Rank and Miss Paget would really go in head down' says Hamlyn. 'I doubt very much if even the biggest firms would take anything like the equivalent bets these days. That sort of on-course betting vanished with the legislation of 1960-61. Those two ladies and a handful of other backers plunged huge amounts and did not by any means always collect. Fortunes changed hands on the course during that era.'

Although Pat Rank had moderated her gambling somewhat by the time Scobie Breasley arrived in England to ride for her husband, she was still a major force in the ring and her temper on any given day may well have depended to a great extent on the state of her betting book at that moment. In any event, it was uncertain and mercurial and Scobie, understandably, saw no good reason why he should tolerate her aggressive attitude.

Scobie was not the only top jockey to experience trouble with Mrs Rank's overbearing manner. Gordon Richards, writing in his autobiography *My Story* which was published in 1955, recounts a visit he made to ride in Ostend during the 1930s when J. V. Rank's horse His Grace was strongly fancied to land the Grand Prix.

Gordon took a party of friends along to make a weekend of it and, after dining well on the Saturday night, they repaired to the local casino to try their luck at the tables. That luck proved to be riding high and the great jockey and his party were still enjoying themselves in the early hours of Sunday morning when in swept the imperious Mrs Rank. 'Richards, don't you think it's about time you were in bed?' she said within the hearing of the entire room. 'We all sat there aghast' Gordon recalls. 'Maybe we were going to bed quite soon but we then changed our minds and it was daylight by the time we did.'

His Grace finished third in the Grand Prix, well beaten by a top-class mare of M. Marcel Boussac's named Correda. But Pat Rank's mischief was not at an end. A few days later, Gordon Richards received a note from J. V. Rank in which the owner stated that he was most disappointed with the running of His Grace in Ostend and that he could not understand the extraordinary way in which his horse had gone out in the betting. This was as good as suggesting that either Richards had not tried to win or that he was unfit to give His Grace a decent ride. Only when Gordon Richards threatened to report the matter to the Jockey Club Stewards was the letter withdrawn and, in fact, destroyed by Mr Rank who had obviously acted foolishly under the influence of his wife.

But despite similar irritations and the problem caused by the Aussie Ring, Scobie's first English season was an undoubted success. He ended the term with 73 victories to his name, a most creditable effort, and on good terms with himself. The great gamble had paid off.

Perhaps the most satisfactory moment, apart from those two early wins at Liverpool, had come with his triumph in Royal Ascot's Hunt Cup. J. V. Rank's five-year-old Hyperbole, well-fancied at 10-1 in a 20-strong field for this highly-competitive handicap, beat the favourite, Wat Tyler, partnered by Scobie's mentor, Gordon Richards.

Breasley signed up with Druid's Lodge again for the 1951 season and took a second retainer with the wealthy owner-breeder Herbert Blagrave, who kept his horses at nearby Beckhampton where he trained them himself. In terms of statistics, Scobie's second English season was slightly less successful than his first, bringing a total of 66 winners. But this was the year during

76

which the Australian had his first taste of Classic race glory.

The 1951 2,000 Guineas was, by common consent, a substandard affair but by winning the Newmarket mile Classic on Ki Ming, Scobie reached an important watershed in his European riding career. Until then, English owners and trainers, while often admiring the Breasley technique, may have tended to regard him as no more than a good jockey in handicaps. Now he was to prove himself a rider with not only the skills but also the temperament to succeed at the very highest level.

Ki Ming had a somewhat curious background. Bred in Ireland, he was a huge 17-hand brown colt by Ballyogan, a sprinter, out of Ulster Lily, a modest handicapper. Not even his most fervent admirer could claim this as anything more than a moderate pedigree. His breeder, J. C. Sullivan, died soon after the big colt was foaled so both Ki Ming and his dam came up for sale in Dublin in the autumn of 1948. Former jump jockey Tim Hyde gave 370 guineas for the yearling while poor old Ulster Lily went for just 50 guineas to another bidder.

The following year, Ki Ming was in the sales ring again – this time at Newmarket's Park Paddocks – and changed hands for 760 guineas. His buyer was trainer John Beary, acting for a Chinese-born restauranteur, Mr Ley On. Ki Ming went into training with Beary and showed an unexpected degree of promise by landing a two-year-old success at Royal Ascot.

But John Beary had lost his licence to train by the end of the 1950 season as the result of a positive dope test on the mare La Joyeuse, taken following an apprentice race at Lingfield Park in which she ran unplaced. In those days, under Jockey Club rules, any trainer automatically forfeited his licence if one of his horses was found to have run with a prohibited substance in its bloodstream. And the Jockey Club's sentence was for an indefinite period.

The sweeping generalization of this regulation, so obviously unfair in some cases, was a scandal. It ran in direct opposition to the British system of justice by presuming guilt without trial, but some years were to pass before the ultra-conservative Jockey Club could be persuaded to take a fairer view by weight of public opinion.

John Beary, who hailed from County Tipperary, was a great hunting man who rode winners both on the Flat and over jumps in his native Ireland and in England before setting up as a trainer in the delightful Sussex village of Alfriston in 1928. He received a large measure of sympathy for his misfortune in the autumn of 1950 with many fellow racing professionals convinced he was the victim of a savage miscarriage of justice. However, John Beary was not allowed to train again until 1953 when he saddled the engagingly-named Loppylugs to win the Cambridge-shire, a highly popular success. He died seven years later at the age of 60.

When the Jockey Club Stewards withdrew Beary's licence, several horses, including Ki Ming, were transferred to his elder brother Michael who had just set up as a trainer at Wantage. Michael Beary had enjoyed a distinguished career in the saddle during which he rode the winners of four Classics – Mid-day Sun in the 1937 Derby, Udaipur (1932 Oaks) and the St Leger heroes Trigo (1929) and Ridge Wood (1949).

Michael Beary lacked the charm and equitable good nature of his younger brother and was so poorly patronised as a trainer that he was obliged to return to riding once more in 1953 when almost 57 years of age. He died virtually broke three years later. But in spite of his shortcomings, Michael Beary was a splendid jockey and a horsemaster of considerable ability who prepared Ki Ming with great care for the 1951 Guineas. Starting at 100-8 but by no means unfancied, the colt, who had once changed hands for just 370 guineas, beat 26 rivals in great style, getting home by a comfortable length and a half from Sir Victor Sassoon's Stokes with Malka's Boy a further short head behind in third place.

Malka's Boy was ridden by Scobie's compatriot Billy 'Last Race' Cook, so named because of his handy habit of winning the final event on the card to help hard-pressed punters out of the mire. Cook enjoyed a good reputation in Australia but English racegoers may not have seen the best of him. Another top Australian jockey to ride in Europe, Edgar Britt, has said of Cook: 'There is no doubt in my mind that if Billy had not suffered unbearable homesickness, he would have made as big a

78

reputation in England as Scobie Breasley. Cook had a perfect seat and was an absolute artist at jumping off in front in long-distance races, slowing the field down and then making a sudden break to steal three or four lengths and stay in front to the post'.

Scobie agrees. 'Billy was a top-class rider, no doubt about that. But he never settled outside Australia for any length of time. Edgar Britt, Rae Johnstone, Bill Williamson, George Moore and a few others gave European racing a fair crack and came to like it, but Billy was always thinking about getting home again.'

Towards the conclusion of the 1951 season Scobie and May Breasley were also beginning to think in terms of quitting England and returning to Australia. Scobie had become rather unsettled, largely because of his on-going feud with Mrs Rank. 'We talked about it a lot, trying to weigh up the good points of staying and the attractions of going back to Melbourne. It was a difficult choice, but in the end we made up our minds to go home. Both Noel Cannon and Mr Rank tried hard to keep me but once the decision was made I was determined.'

Scobie has never been an impulsive man. He likes to sit back and carefully consider his next move. But once that period of consideration is over he very rarely changes his mind. 'I suppose you could say I'm a bit stubborn about some things but when I've made up my mind about anything, right or wrong, I like to see it through.' And see it through he did on this occasion, packing up the Breasley family and their household effects once more for the long trek back to Australia.

Scobie was able to reconstruct his career back home and, as already mentioned, to land another crop of major victories, including that fifth Caulfield Cup triumph. Meanwhile, he bought a plot of land in the fashionable Melbourne suburb of Toorak and put in motion plans to have a new house constructed there. It was a busy time of change with May taking many of the house-building responsibilities on her shoulders while her husband was on the road in his quest for winners.

'I had things well underway', says May. 'In fact, I'd reached the stage of ordering the cooker and God knows what else when Scobie heard from Noel Cannon with a renewed offer for the

What a carve-up! Scobie tackles the suckling pig at a Melbourne party in 1955 on the eve of his return to England. Bill Williamson is on Scobie's left, wearing his celebrated 'Weary Willie' expression.

1953 English season. Then the discussions started all over again.'

James Voase Rank, Scobie's great benefactor, had died at the age of 71 while the Breasleys were en route to Australia but his executors had sold Druid's Lodge to another major figure in English racing, Jack Olding, who was retaining Cannon as trainer there. Cannon had also secured the patronage of 'Lucky' Jack Dewar, a millionaire whisky distiller, whose horses were being sent over from Beckhampton as Noel – later Sir Noel – Murless, who had been in charge of them, was moving to Newmarket.

Cannon was enthusiastic about the new set-up at Druid's Lodge and so keen to bring Scobie back to England that he made a highly lucrative offer with the additional bait of telling his former stable jockey that it would not be necessary for the Breasleys to live down in rural Wiltshire again. 'Live in London, live anywhere you like but do come back' was the message. It was, as the saying goes, an offer too good to refuse so Scobie and May set about cancelling all their plans for that splendid new house in Melbourne and substituting them with one-way tickets to England yet again. But before they could leave there were a thousand and one tasks to be undertaken and Scobie was to be seen rushing round Melbourne selling off the timber and other building materials already assembled on site.

'I sold the land – something May has always maintained was a big mistake because it would have been worth millions of dollars today – the bricks, wood and even the bathroom taps. I got what I paid and that's all I wanted. I'm sure May is right about me losing the chance to make a lot of money but this time I wanted a clean break. We couldn't keep ducking and diving between Australia and England so once the move was on there seemed no point in having property back home. What did I want with bathroom fixtures?

'Everything was a great rush but the prospects in England looked even better than they had done in 1950 and once we had made up our minds I couldn't wait for the off.' Scobie knew that it would seem strange to be back at Druid's Lodge without Mr Rank masterminding the stable. He had grown very fond of this likeable man who had shown him nothing but kindness and

81

'This is where we live now'. May Breasley posing outside the family home at Roehampton in 1958, a photograph taken to illustrate a feature article in an Australian newspaper.

support when he first arrived and who had continued to look after his jockey's interests throughout his brief first stay.

James Rank, born in 1881, was the eldest son of Joseph Rank, a miller from Hull in the East Riding of Yorkshire who made a fortune by modernising flour production methods. J. V. Rank's royal blue and primrose quartered racing colours were first registered in 1920, but he operated on only a small scale for the first 13 years. Then he bought a large number of yearlings at the Doncaster Sales of 1933 and the following year purchased his private stable, Druid's Lodge, appointing Noel Cannon as his trainer in 1935.

After becoming head of the family firm, Mr Rank extended

82

his commercial interests over a wide area, using racing and breeding as a relaxation from the pressures of big business. He was not elected a member of the Jockey Club until some two years before his death despite a keen and active life in racing – both on the Flat and over jumps, his breeding operation and a lifelong passion for coursing.

He left an estate of well over a million pounds but stipulated in his will that only six of the horses in his ownership should be given to his wife. She selected four animals in training and two broodmares, the rest of the Rank string going under the hammer at Newmarket Sales where 83 lots realised 172,560 guineas. Mrs Rank met an unfortunate and mysterious end, falling from a window of her London flat. The riddle of her death was never solved and an open verdict was recorded at the inquest.

John Arthur Dewar, the new power at Druid's Lodge when Scobie Breasley returned there for the start of the 1953 Flat racing season, was another man of vast inherited wealth. He was 39 years of age when his uncle, the first Baron Dewar, died in 1930 leaving him a million and a two-thirds interest in a £2,500,000 trust fund, as well as a string of racehorses together with the Homestall Stud at East Grinstead, on the edge of Ashdown Forest in Sussex. No wonder he was nicknamed 'Lucky' Jack Dewar!

Mr Dewar maintained his uncle's close association with the famous Beckhampton trainer Fred Darling, and the year after Dewar inherited his fortune Darling saddled Cameronian for him to win both the 2,000 Guineas and the Derby.

Lady Juror was among the mares at the Homestall Stud when Jack Dewar took over the estates of his generous relative. She was to play an important role in both the development of his racing fortunes and the riding career of Scobie Breasley. Lady Juror bred Riot, Sansonnet and Fair Trial. Riot's daughter Commotion won a wartime substitute Oaks at Newmarket in 1941, the year Mr Dewar was elected a member of the Jockey Club. Sansonnet was the dam of Tudor Minstrel, winner of the 1947 2,000 Guineas, while Fair Trial sired Festoon, whom Scobie rode to success in the 1954 1,000 Guineas.

9

A Fall from Grace

It was mid-April in 1953 before Scobie Breasley partnered his first winner of the season – Fellermelad at Newbury – but having got off the mark again in England he was soon back in the groove. In fact, the very next day he carried off the Newbury Spring Cup on Prince d'Or, trained at nearby Kingstone Warren by Major Derrick Candy. Major Candy's son, Henry, now handles a top-quality string there including Time Charter, winner of the 1982 Oaks and Champion Stakes and the King George VI and Queen Elizabeth Stakes of 1983. The tall and scholarly Henry Candy received part of his instruction in the training craft from Tommy Smith in Sydney and was also a pupil with C. W. Bartholomew at Chantilly before taking over the Kingstone Warren yard from his father at the end of the 1973 season. He has been turning out a string of major winners ever since.

'That win on Prince d'Or was important', recounts Scobie. 'It seemed to get me going again in England and then I had the thrill of riding a winner for the Queen. Noel Murless asked me to take the mount on Gay Time in the March Stakes at Newmarket because I had ridden the colt as a two-year-old when he was at Druid's Lodge. Gay Time had run second in the previous year's Derby, ridden by Lester Piggott, but had proved disappointing since. Anyway, I managed to get him home at Newmarket for my first victory in the Royal colours. A very exciting moment.'

Gay Time was an unlucky horse. Bred by J. V. Rank out of his mare Daring Miss and an own-brother to those useful performers Elopement and Cash and Courage, this high-quality chestnut won Goodwood's Richmond Stakes and the Solario Stakes at Sandown Park as a two-year-old. When Mr Rank died, Gay

Time was among the horses his wife took over under the stipulation of the millionaire's will. Noel Cannon began to prepare him for the Classics of 1952, the year Scobie was once more riding back home in Australia. Gay Time did not come to hand early and was unfancied and unplaced in the 2,000 Guineas. The race was won by the French-trained Thunderhead II, ridden by Roger Poincelet for the powerful Etienne Pollet stable.

But towards the end of May, Gay Time began to find his true form, winning a minor race at Salisbury, and both Mrs Rank and her trainer came to the conclusion that he should have his chance in the Derby. Noel Cannon engaged 16-year-old Lester Piggott, already making a big name for himself, to partner Gay Time at Epsom. Despite his good juvenile form and that recent success at Salisbury, Gay Time was a 25-1 outsider on Derby Day.

Given a fair rub of the green, he would probably have won and thus enabled Lester Piggott to share with John Parsons the honour of being the youngest jockey to land a Derby, Parsons having been 16 years old when successful on Caractacus in 1862. But the ill-fortune which was to plague Gay Time's career struck him down.

He began by twisting off one of his racing plates in the parade ring and then, during the race itself, met with every kind of trouble. The 1952 Derby is often spoken of as being the roughest big race in living memory and Gay Time certainly met with more than his share of interference. But despite all this, he was beaten only three-parts of a length by the Aga Khan's Tulyar, ridden by that exuberant character Charlie Smirke. After passing the winning post, Gay Time slipped up, deposited his teenage rider on the ground and could not be caught for more than 20 minutes. Piggott wanted to lodge an objection to Tulyar but neither Mrs Rank nor Noel Cannon were at all keen on that idea and talked their jockey out of it.

Opinion is divided on the subject among the experts, but many people continue to hold the view that had Piggott taken his protest before the Epsom stewards, Gay Time might have become the first horse since Aboyeur (1913) to win the Derby on a disqualification.

After his misfortunes in the big race, Mrs Rank moved Gay Time to Walter Nightingall's South Hatch stables at Epsom, overlooking the Derby course and where, incidentally, Scobie Breasley was to train some years later. But Gay Time's luck failed to improve with this change of scene and he was beaten by Tulyar again in the King George VI and Queen Elizabeth Stakes although this time the margin of defeat was only a neck.

Pat Rank had seen enough of her handsome but unlucky colt by now and sold him to the National Stud for £50,000. He was then leased to the Queen for the remainder of his racecourse career and joined Noel Murless at Beckhampton. Gay Time ran poorly in the St Leger but was one of a 68-strong team to move from Beckhampton to Warren Place at Newmarket when Murless transferred his operational headquarters in the autumn of 1952.

Gay Time's form went from bad to worse and his only success as a four-year-old was when Scobie rode him at Newmarket. The National Stud decided to cut their losses and sold Gay Time to Japan where he stood as a stallion until his death at the age of 21 in 1970.

Lester Piggott had only a two-year wait before landing the Derby for the first time on Never Say Die, in 1954. He was still only 18 years old. At the time of writing, Lester has captured the world's most celebrated race on eight subsequent occasions, underlining the claims made on his behalf that he be considered the greatest big-race jockey in the history of world racing.

Never Say Die was trained at Manton by Joe Lawson, who was among the leading horsemasters to patronize Scobie Breasley during the 1953 season. In addition to Lawson and Derrick Candy, Scobie also rode regularly for Fulke Walwyn and had frequent mounts in the colours of the Hon Miss Dorothy Paget, one of the great eccentrics of the Turf who, for reasons known only to herself, invariably referred to the Australian jockey as 'the wretched Breasley'. Scobie's theory for the origin of this odd nickname is that Miss Paget always seemed to think he looked cold and unhappy in the English climate.

'She really was a strange lady', says Scobie. 'I don't think it is any secret that she didn't like men very much. She certainly was very hard to please and changed her trainers, both Flat and

86

National Hunt, so often that you were never quite sure who did have her horses at any particular time. It wasn't until Gordon Richards began training in 1955 that she settled down and left her horses in one place. She certainly trusted Gordon – as everyone does – and it was one of her horses, The Saint, who gave him that all-important first winner as a trainer when he went in at Windsor.'

Scobie's assessment of Dorothy Paget is well-observed. She certainly was a 'strange lady'. Born in 1905, the second daughter of Lord Queenborough by his marriage to the American Pauline Whitney, Miss Paget was so shy that she tried, not with notable success, to hide from life behind a cloak of anonymity or, to be more accurate, a vast grey overcoat of anonymity which hung down to her ankles. On her head, she sported a shapeless blue felt hat, pulled well forward in an attempt to hide her round, pale face from the public gaze. Finding that this Garbo-like disguise made her the focus of public attention on the racecourse rather than helping her to blend into the background, Dorothy Paget came racing less and less frequently during the final years of her life and when she did appear, surrounded herself with a private army of female secretaries and assistants.

Although she owned the great steeplechaser Golden Miller, winner of a Grand National and no fewer than five Cheltenham Gold Cups, Miss Paget had few top-class Flat horses in spite of massive investments in bloodstock. Her blue and yellow colours were carried to success in the war-time substitute Derby of 1943 by Straight Deal but she made a huge loss on her racing investments overall. However, Miss Paget could well afford to indulge herself, not only as a major owner, but also as one of the heaviest gamblers in British racing history.

She lived as a virtual recluse at Chalfont St Giles in Buckinghamshire, keeping well clear of the racing public at large and the racing Press in particular, her habits at home being just as odd as her behaviour on those rare occasions when she ventured out. Time had no meaning for Miss Paget and she liked to eat her main meal of the day during the early hours. Her appetite was immense and once she was seen to consume more than 30 cold lamb cutlets at one of those lonely feasts in the small hours.

When Dorothy Paget died, aged only 55, in 1960, Michael Sobell, later Sir Michael, purchased a large number of her horses-in-training, brood mares and young stock. Mr Sobell was also a patron of Sir Gordon Richards' stable. In partnership with his son-in-law, Lord Weinstock, Sir Michael became one of the most influential owners in British racing while Sir Gordon, having retired from training in 1969, took up the duties of manager to the Sobell-Weinstock horses and fulfilled a similar role for Lady Beaverbrook, widow of the Canadian-born newspaper proprietor.

However, all this was in the uncharted future when Scobie resumed his career in English racing in 1953 and he was glad to ride for the eccentric Miss Paget and others to supplement his retainer for Druid's Lodge.

By the end of that year, Scobie had partnered a total of 84 winners, his best to date. He had also helped celebrate the long overdue Derby triumph of his friend Gordon Richards, whose knighthood had honoured not only himself but the entire community of professional jockeys. 'No one was better pleased to hear of Gordon's recognition by the Queen than May and I', says Scobie. 'And when he won the Derby on Pinza after all those years of trying, it was like a dream come true'.

Breasley was now considered a fixture by English racegoers, many of whom greatly admired the quiet Australian's superb sense of timing and emotionless style. But 1954, having begun in triumph with the 1,000 Guineas victory of Festoon, almost put paid to Scobie's career in England or, for that matter, anywhere else.

Noel Cannon was fully aware that in Festoon he was training a filly of great quality, beauty and well above average ability. But he had no intention of rushing her and Festoon ran only once as a two-year-old, winning a minor six-furlong event worth just £207. Festoon lost her unbeaten tag in the Kempton Park Guineas Trial in the spring of 1954 but there was no panic at Druid's Lodge. Quite the reverse, in fact; confidence grew in her ability as the 1,000 Guineas itself approached. Such confidence was fully justified by events at Newmarket. Given a polished, unhurried ride by Scobie, Festoon won the Classic in fine style, beating Big Berry (Lester Piggott) and Welsh Fairy (Frank Durr) by two lengths and one length. Festoon was well backed at started at odds of 9-2.

'She was a lovely filly to look at and, when she ran in the 1,000 Guineas, a brilliant filly to ride', says Scobie. 'But a mile was as far as she wanted to go and it may have been a mistake to have run her in the Oaks although she was so game that she finished fifth to Sun Cap, ridden by my good friend Rae Johnstone.'

Scobie Breasley was unable to ride Festoon at Epsom because just three days after their joint triumph in the 1,000 Guineas he suffered a fall when the all-too-aptly named Sayonara came down in a minor race at Alexandra Park, the curious track in North London which was shaped like a frying pan. 'It nearly cooked me, that's for sure', recalls Scobie with a grimace of well-remembered pain. 'My eyes were paralysed and I lost all sense of balance. The headaches were dreadful and I was in a pretty sorry state altogether. When you get hurt in a fall, badly hurt that is, you start cheering yourself up by thinking about the good horses you will be riding once you're fit again. But that was something I couldn't do after Sayonara had tipped me off. You see, I wasn't going to be coming back . . .

'Or, at least, that's what the doctors said. They were quite certain about it, not only telling me that my riding career was at an end but that I might not even be able to walk unaided again. It was a really nasty moment because when professional men tell you something like that they have obviously given the matter due thought so you tend to believe what you're told by them. I don't mind admitting to a few minutes of blind panic – blind in more ways than one. But then I started to think about it more calmly. And the more I thought about it, the more determined I became to regain race-riding fitness if I possibly could.

'The type of injuries I suffered that day at Alexandra Park would be less likely to affect a rider in modern times. Back in 1954 jockeys did not wear crash helmets and the ambulance did not follow the field round the course as it does now. Sayonara, a horse of Walter Nightingall's, was in front with me going into the first bend. We had been enjoying a long spell of fine weather but the night before that meeting it had rained hard and this had

Golf is one of Scobie's great relaxations. But once the game played a vital role in helping him regain fitness after doctors had told him never to race-ride again.

made the course at Ally Pally like a skating rink. My filly lost her footing and down we went. The rest of the field galloped on over me but the real damage was done when I hit my head on one of the uprights holding the running rail in place. It proved to be a good deal harder than my head.

'I remember being very sick and feeling a bit embarrassed about it. I was still throwing up when they got me back to the first-aid room and although I had never before suffered a head

90

injury, it was clear that something was very wrong.'

Indeed it was. Scobie had fractured his skull which, in turn, had upset the optic nerves, causing a partial loss of vision and a lack of balance. The accident happened during the first race on the card and by mid-afternoon that same day the jockey was under specialist care at the world-famous London Clinic.

'I remember being in the course first-aid room, feeling rotten but still listening to the public address system. I could hear the next race in progress and make out what was being said around me so at least I knew I hadn't been knocked crackers. But I also knew it was bad. "You're in trouble, Scobie", I was thinking to myself.'

Yet, despite the severity of his injuries which left Scobie with a legacy of discomfort for many months, he was back in the saddle just 12 weeks later. 'I managed to get fit on my own two feet, playing golf every single day for nearly three months. I was lucky to have that fine player Norman Von Nida as a friend. He came out with me a lot to get me started and later I played hole after hole on my own. I must have got to know Wentworth almost as well as the tournament professionals although, I'm sorry to say, it didn't seem to greatly improve my game.

'It wasn't just the golf which put me right in such a short time but all that walking. For a man who earned his living on horse-back, I was doing an awful lot of walking. May said she couldn't understand how I managed it during the first couple of weeks because I was in the habit of falling over at home. I'm sure I played a few air shots.

'But gradually my sense of balance returned to something like normal and so did my co-ordination – both very essential things for a jockey to have in working order. I started to feel stronger again, too, although when I got back to action I still felt a little groggy after the odd hard race. In fact, once or twice I thought I was going to pass out after jumping down and needed to hold on to my horse's mane for a second or two. Nobody seemed to notice – they probably thought I was just patting the horse.'

Alexandra Park racecourse was closed in 1970. 'I rode a fair few winners there but I wasn't all that sad to see it go' says Scobie. 'After all, it nearly finished me off.'

91

With the 1954 season interrupted by this serious injury, Scobie ended the term with only 57 winners to his credit. But he was to top the century in 12 of the next 13 years and to become champion jockey on four occasions, the first rider from outside the British Isles to gain that honour since the American Danny Maher landed the second of his titles in 1913, and the first Australian to do so since Frank Wootton in 1912.

Scobie Breasley has more than a touch of the fatalist in his make-up. But, like all winners in the race of life, he knows that sometimes even the Fates need a tap with the whip to wake them up! Had he taken lying down the verdict of the doctors that his career in racing was at an end following that dreadful Alexandra Park crash, the Turf would have been robbed of those outstanding achievements and British racegoers would never have seen a great jockey in all his mature brilliance.

10

Champion Jockey

The 1954 season saw the retirement from riding of Sir Gordon Richards. Although the great champion had more or less decided to quit the saddle at the conclusion of that year's Flat racing programme, in the end the decision was forced on him by serious injuries sustained in an accident at Sandown Park. The filly Abergeldie reared over backwards leaving the paddock and rolled on Sir Gordon, breaking his pelvis and dislocating four ribs. It was the end of an era. Gordon Richards had been riding since 1920 and had partnered 4,870 winners from 21,843 mounts in Great Britain. He had been champion jockey an unprecedented 26 times.

For more than a quarter of a century the swaggering little man from Shropshire, whose modesty utterly belied his appearance, had been a sporting legend, thousands of racing fans backing his every mount secure in the knowledge that Gordon was always a trier. Gordon Richards was, in short, a public idol and not even Lester Piggott has managed to replace him in terms of public esteem.

Scobie, who had ridden against Sir Gordon in the keenest rivalry since his arrival from Australia while enjoying the benefits of his distinguished opponent's firm friendship, was greatly distressed by the painful injuries Richards suffered. 'My own unhappy experience at Alexandra Park made me realise just what Gordon was going through', Scobie remembers. 'But in his case it was worse. I was able to come back but this was the end for Gordon as a jockey – such a sad end to such a wonderful career.'

Noel Murless approached Scobie to become his stable jockey on Sir Gordon's retirement, an offer which Scobie regarded as a singular compliment. 'For me, a comparative newcomer to

English racing, to be given the chance of stepping into Gordon's boots was nothing short of an honour. But we were living at Roehampton in South London then and I neither wanted to uproot my home again nor to travel up to Newmarket two or three days a week in order to ride work.

'When I turned down the Murless job it was offered to Lester Piggott who accepted and rode with tremendous success for the Warren Place stable for 11 years. History repeated itself in the 1980s when Lester went back there to ride as first jockey for Henry Cecil, Sir Noel's son-in-law. Not many people know that I was offered the Warren Place job before Lester, but although he had any number of good horses to ride there over the years I have no regret about declining the move because it was to lead to my long and very happy association with Gordon Richards as a trainer.

'Gordon started training at Beckhampton, the yard Noel Murless had vacated, in 1955 with Jock Wilson as his stable jockey but the following year, with a string of 50 horses, he moved up the road to Martin Hartigan's old stable at Ogbourne Maizey and I took over as his first-choice rider. This was a move very much to my liking, specially after I had been down to have a look at the horses and seen their potential, but the hardest thing was to tell Noel Cannon that I would be leaving Druid's Lodge.

'Noel Cannon was one of the nicest men in racing, a real gentleman in fact, and the success of my career in England owed a great deal to him. He was a most able trainer. Leaving his stable was all the more difficult when, in response to the news that I intended to take up Sir Gordon's offer, Noel said he would increase my retainer at Druid's Lodge. This offer was, as it happened, worth more money than Gordon Richards was paying me, but money is not everything and I had made up my mind. Noel Cannon took the decision well and we remained friends. I still rode for him whenever I was free, including taking the mount on Sarcelle who won the Imperial Produce Stakes and the Cheveley Park in 1956. Noel always said she was the best two-year-old he ever handled and she headed the Free Handicap weights.

'Eventually, Jack Purtell came over from Australia to replace me and won the Champagne Stakes at Doncaster on Jack Olding's colt Kelly. Unfortunately, although Noel was perfectly satisfied with the riding of Jack Purtell, he didn't get much patronage over here and was denied the opportunities his ability warranted.

'My judgement of Gordon's horses proved to be pretty sound, and in our first season together we had a notable success with Pipe of Peace in the Middle Park Stakes. This colt was owned by the Greek shipping man Stavros Niarchos who is now more active than ever as an owner with a big string of horses shared out between trainers in England, France and Ireland. I ended the 1956 season with 143 winners and realised that, with any luck, the title might soon be within reach. I had accepted second and third retainers from Jack Clayton at Newmarket and Staff Ingham at Epsom so had an ample choice of decent rides, not to mention the "spares" which always come along when a jockey is doing well and has become fashionable.

'My association with Jack Clayton was particularly happy. He was always both pleasant and helpful and didn't demand that I keep trekking up to Newmarket to ride gallops. In fact, just about the only time I rode work on his horses was those occasions when I was already up at Headquarters for a race meeting. Then, he would come up to me and ask if I could possibly fit in a gallop session or two in such a way it seemed I was doing him a real favour. You would never have thought from his manner that I was being paid a retainer by his stable. I rode for Jack Clayton for more than ten years – very happy years, too.

'About that time I acquired yet another string to my bow when the Duke and Duchess of Norfolk began putting me up on their horses trained at Arundel. They both understood racing and jockeyship wonderfully well, never tying me down with complicated pre-race instructions and never making a complaint if a fancied horse was beaten. Jockeys would have a much easier time if all owners were like the late Duke and Lavinia, Duchess of Norfolk.

'I became champion jockey of England for the first time in 1957, a great thrill and the final realisation of all those dreams I had brought with me from Australia seven years before. May

95

and I now looked upon England as our home. We had been shown both friendship and understanding by the great majority of English racing professionals and ordinary racegoers alike. A great many Australians think the English a bit snobbish, difficult people to get to know. With a few exceptions, that was never our experience and to be acclaimed champ in a country which stages the most competitive racing in the world made our decision to leave Australia 100 per cent worthwhile.'

Scobie's 1957 total of 173 winners halted Doug Smith's run of three consecutive championships yet, from a Classic race point of view, it was a frustrating season both for the Australian jockey and for Sir Gordon Richards. Pipe of Peace finished third to Crepello in both the 2,000 Guineas and the Derby, while Court Harwell was beaten just a length into second place by Ballymoss in the St Leger.

Noel Murless trained Crepello for Sir Victor Sassoon, the big chestnut colt's breeder. Had Scobie accepted the retainer Murless offered him two years earlier he, rather than Lester Piggott, would have ridden to victory in the 1957 Derby, a victory which saw Crepello acclaimed as one of the outstanding Epsom winners of the century.

Unhappily, the horse's soundness was no match for his ability and he was never able to race again after his Derby triumph. Murless was already experiencing some difficulty with Crepello's forelegs when this great colt beat Ballymoss and Pipe of Peace for the Derby, and two months later he broke down so badly on his off-fore that he was at once retired to stud. Crepello made a considerable impact as a stallion, breeding Mysterious (1,000 Guineas and Oaks), Celina (Irish Oaks) and Crepellana (French Oaks) in addition to that high-quality colt Busted and a stack of other notable horses. Crepello's daughter Bleu Azur was the dam of Altesse Royale, winner of the 1,000 Guineas, Oaks and Irish Oaks. His stud career ended in 1974 and he had to be put down soon afterwards.

Ballymoss, it is widely accepted, would have won nine out of ten Derbys but Vincent O'Brien's colt, due to play an important part in Scobie Breasley's career as an international jockey the following year, took full advantage of Crepello's premature retirement to win the St Leger and so give his now legendary trainer the first of many English Classic successes.

'Pipe of Peace was a decent sort of horse, consistent and willing', recalls Scobie. 'He might well have been good enough to win a Classic in an average year, but neither Crepello nor Ballymoss could be called average rivals. In fact, both were champions or, at least, Crepello was a champion and Ballymoss was to become one as a four-year-old. In any case, Pipe of Peace was a bit unlucky at Epsom, running into some interference in the straight.

'Vincent O'Brien was only just beginning to make his name as a Flat trainer at that time after his outstanding achievements with jumpers. Tommy Burns always rode Ballymoss but he was hurt in a fall in Ireland in the Spring of 1958 and O'Brien telephoned to ask if I would partner the previous year's Derby runner-up in the Coronation Cup. Naturally, I was happy to oblige.

'Ballymoss started an even-money favourite in a field of only five. I tracked Fric and Jean Deforge round Tattenham Corner and then let Ballymoss run. He had them cold in a few strides and won impressively by a couple of lengths. It was the start of a great partnership between us.'

Indeed it was. Together Ballymoss and Scobie went on to win the Eclipse Stakes, the King George VI and Queen Elizabeth Stakes and the Prix de l'Arc de Triomphe. All three of those races – a collective highlight in Scobie's career – are worthy of discussion but first Ballymoss himself and his racecourse performances as a whole must be put into perspective.

Vincent O'Brien came to the Tattersalls' St Leger sales at Doncaster in 1955 with two objects in mind, namely the purchase of a few suitable yearlings and, more ambitious, to find an owner wealthy enough to pay their training bills. Although the Irishman had saddled Chamier to win the Irish Derby two years earlier, he was still regarded as a National Hunt trainer. But O'Brien had already decided to make the switch from jumping to the Flat and his trip to Doncaster was to prove successful in a way which not even he could have foretold.

While at the sales he was introduced to an American named

97

A mud-caked Scobie thanks Ballymoss after their victory in the 1958 Prix de l'Arc de Triomphe. The great Irish-trained horse seems unimpressed.

John McShain who was on the lookout for a European trainer willing to handle his horses. The outcome of this meeting was that O'Brien bought five yearlings on Mr McShain's behalf. All were to win races and one of their number, the deep-girthed chestnut by Lord Derby's stallion Mossborough, subsequently to be named Ballymoss, was to become the first of the great international champions to be trained at Ballydoyle House, Vincent O'Brien's hideaway in the Golden Vale of County Tipperary.

Ballymoss was out of a mare named Indian Call, 18 years of age at the time this future champion was foaled and who, in any case, had a modest record for producing winners. But O'Brien

98

was already developing his uncanny knack of viewing an un-furnished young horse and being able to envisage that same animal as a mature racer. Ballymoss was knocked down to him at just 4,500 guineas – one of the greatest sales ring bargains of all time. By the time Ballymoss retired from the racecourse his prize-money earnings amounted to more than £107,000 – a massive figure in those days – and he was eventually sold on to become a stallion for a further £250,000.

As a two-year-old, Ballymoss was so backward that O'Brien was obliged to exercise great patience. He did manage to win a maiden plate worth just £202 at Leopardstown but hardly looked a superstar in the making. But Ballymoss, rather like a fine wine, improved with keeping. And when he carried off the mile and a half Trigo Stakes back at Leopardstown in the early part of the 1957 season, some shrewd backers began to support the O'Brien colt for the Derby.

It seems doubtful that Ballymoss would ever have beaten Crepello, but his cause was not aided by a foot injury which meant the colt missing a couple of pre-Derby gallops. O'Brien warned Mr McShain that his colt would not be 100 per cent for the Epsom Classic and on the strength of that message McShain cancelled his proposed visit to England.

Ballymoss ran Crepello to a length and a half, a splendid performance in the circumstances, and went on to land the Irish Derby with ease. Beaten in York's Great Voltigeur Stakes, he upheld the Derby form by beating Court Harwell in the St Leger. Ballymoss disappointed in the Champion Stakes but his true value as a four-year-old was there for all to see.

If his Coronation Cup win required little effort, how much more comfortable was Ballymoss's success in the Eclipse? Unleashed by Scobie two furlongs from the post, the odds-on favourite stretched smoothly clear to beat the three-year-old Restoration by six lengths – a most un-Breasleylike distance.

Ascot's King George VI and Queen Elizabeth Stakes found Ballymoss faced with stronger opposition including Derby win-ner Hard Ridden. Consequently, he started odds-against this time but the outcome was just the same. Once again, Scobie kicked passing the two-furlong marker and Ballymoss came home on the bit with three lengths to spare over Almeria with Hard Ridden back in sixth place.

Arc de Triomphe day in 1958 was dismal. Early morning drizzle turned into a downpour as racegoers made their way down the Bois de Boulogne towards Longchamp. Hats and hairstyles suffered; so did the confidence of Ballymoss supporters since the great Irish champion, despite his victory in the soft at Doncaster the previous Autumn, was reputed not to be at his best when the ground was riding heavy. But it has been truly said that outstanding horses can tackle any conditions and Ballymoss, ridden with both dash and kindness by Scobie, beat his old rival Fric by a couple of lengths with 15 others strung out behind.

Scobie, escorted on both sides by mounted French policemen, returned to unsaddle Ballymoss in triumph. For once, his calm gave way to jubilation. 'May tells me I was so excited that I was waving my whip above my head like a lunatic. I suppose I needed to find some use for it – there was certainly no need for me to touch Ballymoss at any stage of the race.'

But even amid all these celebrations Scobie remembered to send an apology via Rae Johnstone to French jockey Max Garcia. 'I had a very good run through the race until the home turn but then came one of those nasty moments when it looked as though Ballymoss would get shut in on the rails. I needed to squeeze through and that did no favours to Garcia who was riding that fine filly Bella Paola, winner of the 1,000 Guineas at Newmarket earlier in the year. I speak no French so I got Rae to tell him I was sorry. He sent a message back to tell me not to worry – he would have done just the same thing given the chance.'

Ballymoss thus completed a remarkable grand slam and an elated Vincent O'Brien decided to run him once more in the Washington International at Laurel in Maryland, then the top American invitation grass race which had been inaugurated in 1952. 'Unfortunately, that's when the Ballymoss fairy story turned into a nightmare', Scobie Breasley says.

11

An International Incident

The ease of jet travel has led to a proliferation of major international races in recent years. Owners and trainers of high-quality racehorses now send their champions on prize-money-seeking missions around the world for such events as Canada's Rothmans International at Woodbine Park in Toronto, the Budweiser Million at Arlington Park in Chicago or even Tokyo's Japan Cup. But back in the 1950s the Washington International, staged at Laurel in Maryland, had this sphere of racing activity all to itself.

The Washington International, the brainchild of Laurel president John D. Schapiro, was run for the first time in 1952 and won by the English-owned and trained Wilwyn, ridden by the late Manny Mercer, elder brother of Joe. By the time Ballymoss was being aimed at the 1958 race, the Washington International was fully established and any owner considered an approach from Schapiro to run his or her horse in this invitation-only spectacular a decided honour. The ten starters in 1958 represented seven different countries. In addition to the host nation there were runners from Australia, West Germany, The Argentine, Venezuela, Ireland and Russia.

It is doubtful if any race has attracted a wider spread of international Turf interests but, following his series of highly-impressive major victories in Europe, Ballymoss was considered, on both sides of the Atlantic, likely to win. Just why he failed was then, and still remains, a decidedly contentious issue on which opinions are sharply divided. The view of Scobie Breasley, rider of Ballymoss and therefore surely better situated to judge than anyone else, has never before been documented in any detail.

The bald facts are these: Ballymoss was utterly unsuited to the cramped and turning Laurel track, had an unfortunate run

The jockeys who competed in the 1958 Washington International at Laurel, among them four of the greatest riders in racing history. In the back row are Bill Shoemaker (second left), Lester Piggott (third left) and Scobie Breasley (far right), and in the front is Eddie Arcaro (second left).

in what is generally accepted as being a rough and unsatisfactory race and could finish only third behind Tudor Era and Sailor's Guide, the former being relegated to second place for causing interference after the Laurel Stewards had seen the film of the event. The official American form book version of how Bally-moss ran reads this way: 'Raced in contention from the start; was bothered when Orsini II hit him just before completing a turn; recovered and remained a factor until nearing the stretch then drifted wide and failed to respond to pressure.'

102

But that tells only half the story, according to Scobie. 'The day before the race, Vincent O'Brien and I watched some films of previous runnings of the Washington International and I told O'Brien that, judging by what we had seen, there seemed to be very little, if any, interference during races at Laurel', Scobie says. 'Although the track looked tight for a horse like Ballymoss, I was happy that, given a clear passage, he would have every chance of winning. I recall saying as much to O'Brien and to several other people. Before I went out to mount the trainer turned to me and said "I've done my bit, now it's up to you".

'But the race was never going our way. Orsini II, ridden by Lester Piggott, ran into the hedge – they had hedges rather than rails at Laurel – and hit Ballymoss, turning my mount sideways on. Lester told me afterwards that the sun was in his eyes and that he couldn't see where he was going. I don't know if that was a genuine excuse or not, but the antics of Lester and his horse certainly upset Ballymoss and he was never really going on an even keel afterwards.

'He got back into the race but met interference again on the final turn and that's why he swung wide and could never get on terms with the first two. In all the circumstances, Ballymoss ran pretty well. It was a pity he was beaten but it was hardly my fault. In any case, even before the race, John Hislop told May that, in his view, Ballymoss did not look the same horse as the one he had seen race in England. John, the man who bred Brigadier Gerard, is a greatly respected judge of a horse and may have seen something not quite right about Ballymoss. We're never likely to know now, but the reaction to his defeat from both Vincent O'Brien and Mr McShain was hurtful and unjust to me.

'Neither Mr McShain nor his wife put in an appearance after the race and O'Brien, while he did come down as I was unsaddling, left the course immediately afterwards. Eventually I got a message to say, in effect, would I tell the American racing Press that it was my fault Ballymoss was beaten. Of course, I was not prepared to say any such thing. I was never again offered a ride on any horse in the McShain colours, but still hold the view that I was in no way to blame for what happened at

103

Laurel, so it would have been quite wrong for me to shoulder the responsibility.

'No one was more unhappy than I that a great racehorse's career should end on such a sad note. I believe that Ballymoss was not only a true champion but the best horse I ever rode. He gave me a tremendous thrill by winning the Arc and I certainly didn't think the whole thing would turn sour so soon after that great day in Paris.'

Scobie considers his ride on Ballymoss in the United States stands regrettable comparison with his ongoing misfortunes in the Melbourne Cup. But those races amount only to rare blemishes on an otherwise supremely successful career as an international jockey of the highest standard. 'I suppose every rider has his bogey events', reasons Breasley. 'Lester, for example, has never won the Lincoln or the Cambridgeshire. And it took Gordon Richards countless rides before he managed to win the Derby. It's a matter of being offered the right horse and then having the right luck in running. Riding races from the grandstand has always been easier than actually being out there on the horse's back.

'There is so little time to think and act during a race but mistaken tactics always look so obvious afterwards when you watch a film or video of what happened. In slow motion it becomes clearer still where and how things have gone wrong but race-riding is, if you like, the art of the instant decision. Sometimes those reflex moves are right but almost as often they are wrong. But you cannot steer half a ton of horseflesh by computer. You simply make your choice and go – hoping that it will pan out. I can look back on any number of races and think "if only . . ." but there's not a lot of point in doing that. I suppose one way of deciding between great jockeys and just good jockeys is that the great ones lose fewer races they should have won than the others.'

Ballymoss, who had cost, you will recall, just 4,500 guineas as a yearling, won a total of £107,165 in stakes, so eclipsing the British prize-money record which had been held by the 1952 Derby winner, Tulyar. He was hardly as good a stallion as he had been a racehorse, but did get the 1967 Derby winner, Royal Palace, becoming leading sire that season. He was also responsible for Merry Mate (Irish Guinness Oaks), Ancasta (Irish Guinness Oaks), Ballyboy (German St Leger) and Parmelia (Ribblesdale Stakes).

Scobie paid only one further visit to Laurel when unplaced on Apostle II in the 1960 Washington but, by contrast, Lester Piggott's return journeys to Maryland have proved highly fruitful. Lester carried off the 1968 race on Derby hero Sir Ivor – trained by Vincent O'Brien – and was first again the following year when partnering Karabas who thus became the first English-trained winner since Wilwyn in the inaugural year. Lester captured his third Washington International when Argument scored for France in 1980.

John D. Schapiro was a visionary in terms of global racing and while his event can no longer match some of its imitators for prize-money and, consequently, prestige these days, the Washington International remains a highly-acclaimed event.

There is no doubt that jockeys, in common with other professional sportsmen who enjoy the status and high material rewards associated with success throughout the world, have enviable life-styles. But the pressures are great – and growing.

Sometimes, in the heat of a major race, those reflex actions of which Scobie Breasley has spoken can alter the value of a potential stallion or broodmare by many thousands – even millions – of pounds. The difference between winning a Derby or an Arc de Triomphe by a short head or losing by an equally narrow margin can be frightening in an age when a top stallion property, his stud potential backed up by a win in such races, may amount to as much as £20,000,000, placing jockeys in a position few would envy.

At the Keeneland Select Yearling Sales in Kentucky last year the value of bloodstock as an international commodity speculation reached an all-time – some might say – absurd level when Sheikh Mohammed Al Maktoum gave $10,200,000 for a son of the great Canadian stallion Northern Dancer. If this colt, now in training at John Dunlop's Castle Stables at Arundel in Sussex, were to win, for the sake of argument, the 1985 Derby, his dollar value would have so many digits it might be mistaken for a computer read-out.

105

So spare a thought for the jockey entrusted with a big-race mount on a horse of this calibre. An error of judgement on just such a vital occasion could knock several noughts off his stud valuation. Jockeys are highly rewarded for their skills. Only top tournament golf professionals and tennis players can be compared in the earnings tables among the superstars of sport. But their responsibility, and therefore their professional ability and temperament, is under the microscope of intense public scrutiny virtually on a daily basis.

No wonder many of them become withdrawn, almost taciturn, when questioned by racing enthusiasts who follow their favourites with the interest and devotion that others reserve for film stars or pop idols. In fact, very few jockeys mix freely with people from outside the closely-knit and somewhat sheltered world of the racing professional. They tend to be mistrustful of strangers and wary with those who express a perfectly natural level of inquisitiveness.

'It's a serious business – it has to be with so much money at stake', Scobie points out. 'I'm sure that jockeys get just as much fun out of life as any other group of people but there is no doubt that racing, by its very nature, is a rather secretive business. A blabbermouth doesn't last long in racing so you learn to say as little as possible to as few a people as possible without being rude.'

Yarn-swapping, practical-joking and party-going tend to be activities confined to within the riding community itself or to a handful of carefully-chosen and trusted close friends. However, this does not mean to say that, within these limitations, jockeys are unable to let their hair down.

Many of the top riders in Britain at the present time could be called 'characters' in every sense of the word. Willie Carson, with his infectious grin and baying laugh, Greville Starkey, whose impersonation of a barking terrier is so perfect that his fellow jockeys are guaranteed to look for a canine intruder no

Opposite: *Scobie pictured with the Queensland-born jockey Neville Sellwood in 1961. The following year, having ridden Larkspur to win the Derby, Sellwood was killed in a fall at Maisons-Laffitte. He was 39 years of age.*

matter how often he pulls this particular trick, and that quietly humorous little Irishman Richard Fox are among those always ready to enliven the weighing-room. Even Lester Piggott, he of the frozen public image, is a witty and irreverent storyteller, capable of delighting his friends with jokes, usually to the discomfort of some rival.

But just watch the smiles fade and the banter dry up at the appearance of a 'Connaught' on the scene. (The term 'Connaught', short for Connaught Ranger, is racing slang for stranger.) This insular state of affairs is widespread on the Turf and probably explains why so many jockeys marry within the racing community. Perhaps there is less tight-lipped and closed-rank behaviour these days than was once the general rule, but it still exists to a noticeable degree.

'It was certainly a golden rule during my days as an apprentice that stable secrets must be closely guarded', Scobie Breasley says. 'And no trainer likes to think that the prospects of any of his horses are being discussed by members of his staff – and that certainly includes jockeys. Of course, professional punters and bookmakers have always had their contacts in stables and no doubt they always will, but people who make a habit of passing stable information are on very thin ice.

'I suppose this is the basic reason why jockeys normally keep things to themselves – they were all taught to do so from the start. Those early lessons stay with you even if you become a big-name jockey or a top trainer. In fact, if anything, you become less talkative as you get older as by that time you are only too aware that there are a lot of people around who don't want your friendship so much as a way of picking your brains or getting you to pass on what you may know about your own horses or someone else's.

'We may seem a bit stand-offish sometimes, but that's the reason why.'

Opposite: *Scobie, who loves children, pictured playing with his granddaughter Zonda, 19 months old at the time.*

12

The Blacksmith's Derby

It was a quiet Spring evening in May, 1966 when Scobie Breasley received an unexpected telephone call at his home in Roehampton. The caller was Gordon Smyth, in his first season as a public trainer at Heath House, Lewes. Smyth's to-the-point question: 'Do you have a ride in the Derby?'

Scobie told his caller: 'I'm not committed, why?' Gordon Smyth stunned Scobie by asking: 'Would you like the mount on Charlottown?'

Scobie recalls every syllable of that short conversation for the very good reason that it had a highly embarrassing sequel with his long-time friend, Australian compatriot and weighing-room rival, Ron Hutchinson, then stable jockey to the Smyth yard. Scobie remembers that subsequent call with matching clarity.

Hutchinson: 'Hey Scobie, I've lost the Derby ride on Charlottown.'
Breasley: 'I know. I ride it.'
Hutchinson: 'What do you mean, Scobes?'
Breasley: 'Gordon Smyth rang and asked if I had a ride in the Derby. I told him I didn't. He asked if I wanted to ride Charlottown and I told him I did.'
Hutchinson: 'Bloody hell, Scobes.'
Breasley: 'Look Ron, I asked why you didn't ride and Smyth said the owners don't want you any more. There's no way you ride the horse at Epsom so I might as well.'
Hutchinson: 'Bloody hell, Scobes.'

Greatly to the credit of Ron Hutchinson, he took no lasting offence at being replaced on the colt who gave Scobie his second Derby triumph for, as Breasley had quite rightly stated, Sir

Harold and Lady Zia Wernher, the owners of Charlottown, had decided to dispense with Hutchinson's services and that decision was final.

Ron Hutchinson, invariably referred to by Scobie as 'the little fellow', by virtue of the fact that Breasley claims a half-inch height advantage, had ridden Charlottown in the Lingfield Derby Trial and, to be frank, was some way short of his best on that occasion. To dismiss a distinguished jockey for one indifferent performance may seem harsh, but is any owner's undoubted prerogative. It was a prerogative the Wernhers decided to exercise.

Consequently, Scobie was off to Lewes the following week to ride Charlottown in a pre-Derby gallop. He liked what he found. Charlottown gave the great Australian rider that indefinable but unmistakable 'feel' which only a quality horse provides.

The Derby of 1966 lacked any cross-Channel competition as an outbreak of swamp fever in France had resulted in a travel ban being imposed by the racing authorities. Had Charlottown been subjected to European rivals he might not have won at Epsom. By general acceptance he does not rate among the best post-war Derby winners but, in fairness, he could do no more than beat the best available opponents of his year.

But there were to be two further dramas before Charlottown paddled to victory on a pouring-wet afternoon which reduced Derby-day finery to so much bedraggled pulp.

Before Lingfield, Charlottown had suffered an injury to his off-fore leg and there was a slight reccurrence only days before the Derby. Trainer Smyth, a man renowned for his calmness and far more likely to be worried about his golf swing than the vagaries which beset the training craft, showed concern on this occasion.

Smyth had taken over the Heath House yard from Jack 'Towser' Gosden early in 1966 when the latter was obliged to retire due to ill health. Charlottown, unbeaten in three starts as a two-year-old, was part and parcel of the deal. Jack Gosden, a brilliant trainer of the old school with a string of carefully-planned and executed handicap coups to his credit, lived long

111

enough to know that Charlottown had won the Derby although he was not well enough to attend the big race.

Much of the merit for Charlottown's success rested with Gosden who had 'made' the horse. It was a pity that the onset of of cancer prevented him from one further year of training but Gordon Smyth's role was, it should not be forgotten, equally vital, not least because he had the uncommon good sense to take the Lewes farrier, George Windless, to Epsom with him on Derby day.

Charlottown, apparently fully recovered from his slight training set-back, had another and more permanent problem – thin-soled feet which made him very difficult to shoe. While parading in those monsoon conditions at Epsom he lost his off-fore racing plate. This was just the sort of event Smyth had feared but with his blacksmith on call the tricky re-plating process was undertaken while the other Derby runners circled the paddock for an extra ten minutes in the unrelenting rain.

'It was a bad time for all of us' Scobie Breasley remembers. 'Charlottown's feet were like shells and one tiny slip by the blacksmith would have put him out of the Derby. Just think of the pressure that man was under. Backroom boys like him very rarely get any praise but Charlottown would certainly not have won but for his skill and calmness.'

The following day, a national newspaper summed up the tense pre-race drama by announcing: 'Derby winner Charlottown, owned by Lady Zia Wernher, trained by Gordon Smyth, ridden by Scobie Breasley and shod by George Windless.'

Another tribute to this outstanding example of the farrier's art was the fact that Charlottown's famous off-fore plate not only stood the test imposed by the Derby itself but remained firmly in place for a further three weeks. The 1966 Derby has carried into racing folklore several epithets, among them the 'Pac-a-Mac Derby' and the 'Downpour Derby' but perhaps the 'Blacksmith's Derby' is more apt.

Opposite: *Epsom 1966, and another Derby for Scobie. The great Australian jockey forces home Charlottown (right) to gain a photo-finish verdict over Pretendre (Paul Cook).* (S & G Press Agency Ltd)

Despite the absence of the French, a field of 25 started belatedly with Charlottown towards the rear to half distance although the pace was poor. In fact, Scobie's mount had only three members of this big Derby field behind him after covering the first half mile but this position, unpromising as it looked from the stands, was part of Scobie's pre-race plan. 'I wanted the rails – I always wanted the rails – and in order to secure that position it was necessary to stay back in the early stages.'

Breasley's tactics were, once again, to pay a rich dividend. Gradually he improved Charlottown's position without leaving the inside rail for a single stride. The Lewes colt had little room rounding Tattenham Corner in sixth place but Breasley held tenaciously to the inner while somehow managing to avoid being baulked by his closely packed rivals. It was rather like the Red Sea parting for the staff of Moses. Once in line for home, Right Noble, the leader, began to weaken, leaving an obligingly wide gap for Charlottown to slip through. Half a furlong later Black Prince II followed suit, although the space between Jimmy Lindley's mount and the rails was far narrower. 'Not much room but just enough', Scobie Breasley remembers with one of those engaging grins.

Racing into the final furlong, Charlottown still had about half a length to make up on Pretendre, just preferred to Scobie's colt in the betting and the mount of 20-year-old Paul Cook. The sandy-haired Gloucestershire lad rode hard and well but he was undoubtedly out-manoeuvred and out-thought by the Australian master jockey that day. In the last 100 yards Breasley sat down to ride one of his strongest finishes and Charlottown responded with great courage to win a thrilling, if moderate, Derby by a neck with Black Prince II, his Lingfield Trial conqueror, five lengths further back in third place and Sodium – a horse destined to play an important role in Charlottown's future career – fourth.

As May Breasley hurried down from her place in the stand she lost a shoe in the crush, an extraordinary coincidence coming just 20 minutes after Charlottown's loss of that famous racing plate in the parade ring.

Charlottown had been bred by the Wernhers at their Someries Stud. He was a smallish bay colt by the Prix du Jockey-Club and

114

Scobie Breasley astride the victorious Charlottown.

Grand Prix de Paris winner Charlottesville out of that outstanding racemare Meld who was by Alycidon. Meld, foaled in 1952, lived to the ripe old age of 31. It is only proper to digress briefly and pay tribute to this remarkable equine lady.

Lady Zia Wernher placed Meld with Cecil Boyd-Rochfort at Newmarket when she came into training in 1954 but, unfortunately, she split a pastern so her debut was postponed until late in the September of that year when she started completely unfancied but finished second to her stable-mate Corporal. It was to prove her only defeat.

Meld's brilliance as a three-year-old was unquestioned. During 1955 she carried off a remarkable 1,000 Guineas-Oaks-

115

St Leger treble, only the sixth filly in racing history to achieve that triple-Classic grand slam and preceded only by Pretty Polly (1904) and Sun Chariot (1942) this century.

Ridden to all her triumphs by Harry Carr, father-in-law of 1979 champion jockey Joe Mercer, Meld also carried off Royal Ascot's Coronation Stakes. The Royal meeting that year was postponed until July because of a national rail strike since 30 years ago the vast majority of racegoers travelled by train. It was simply a postponement of the inevitable so far as the unbeatable Wernher filly was concerned.

Meld won both the 1,000 Guineas and Oaks with commanding ease, but there were scares both before and during the 1955 St Leger.

The great filly was odds-on for the Doncaster Classic but that race was run in the midst of a bad coughing epidemic. Cecil Boyd-Rochfort, later knighted for his services to British racing, kept Meld in isolation but there were rumours – probably well founded – that Meld had coughed twice on St Leger morning.

Harry Carr, believing that Meld was sickening for the virus, attempted to ride her with the utmost tenderness and consideration but Lester Piggott, never a man to spurn an offering by the Fates, drove Nucleus in pursuit of the favourite just as Meld had quickened to dismiss the challenge of the French raider Beau Prince. Carr was obliged to go for his whip and although Meld responded most gallantly she drifted towards the rails and Piggott had to switch Nucleus in order to maintain his bid. Meld held on by just three-quarters of a length but Piggott immediately lodged an objection for crossing.

The objection was not only overruled but Lester forfeited his deposit – £10 in those days – as the Doncaster Stewards considered his complaint to be frivolous. I suspect that it would have been treated more sympathetically by contemporary Stewards, but Piggott would have been the least popular man in racing had Meld been disqualified.

Opposite: *Trainer Gordon Smyth congratulates his 1966 Derby winner. Leading Charlottown in is Michael Jarvis, now himself a successful Newmarket trainer.* (S & G Press Agency Ltd)

When her St Leger victory was confirmed Cecil Boyd-Rochfort became the first English trainer to win a million pounds in stakes for the patrons of his stable. Sir Cecil died at his home in Ireland in 1983 at the age of 95. Judged by current standards, Meld's contribution of £43,051 seems paltry but it was a significant figure for the mid-1950s.

The St Leger success was thrown into true relief only a few hours after the race, when Meld began to cough repeatedly and to run a high temperature. Unfortunately, Meld proved a disappointing brood mare with the exception of producing Charlottown, although another of her sons, the maiden Mellay, by the first of Lester Piggott's Derby winners, Never Say Die, subsequently became a highly-successful stallion in New Zealand.

Scobie Breasley saw plenty of Meld from the rear during 1955. He partnered Feria to finish third in that year's 1,000 Guineas and was on Reel In when she was beaten a total of nine lengths in the Oaks. 'Meld was a lovely big filly who could really gallop', says Scobie. 'I was always looking at her hind quarters because the fillies I was riding were never good enough to get upsides of such a brilliant racemare.'

Opposite: *Scobie and May Breasley off for a well-earned winter holiday in Barbados after the Australian had won the 1963 jockeys' championship by a single winner from Lester Piggott.*

118

13

On the Gravy Train

The curt dismissal of Scobie Breasley after his 1964 Derby win on Santa Claus undoubtedly left a bitter taste. His triumph on Charlottown, widely acclaimed by the racing public, was better received by that colt's owners but their appreciation of a fine Epsom ride did not extend to a cash bonus!

Scobie and his wife were, in the fullness of time, summoned to appear for lunch at Sir Harold and Lady Zia Wernher's stately home, Luton Hoo in Bedfordshire. 'I remember saying to May that we could expect a nice present to be discreetly passed across the dining-room table on a silver platter' says Scobie. 'What I really thought was that I was first in the queue for a bloody great cheque.

'Lunch with the Wernhers was quite an experience with May and I waiting for the big moment. What a let-down. "I have something for you," says Her Ladyship and hands over a gravy-boat – silver plated, too. Quite nice but not quite what I had expected for winning the Derby. I think May swapped it for a couple of candlesticks or something. I suppose people as rich as that have little sense of value.'

Breasley's strictly token gift must have looked all the more insignificant as it was handed over in the opulent surroundings of Luton Hoo, a grand if rather curious mansion stacked with the works of Titian, Rembrandt, Rubens and Hals by Sir Harold's father, Sir Julius Wernher, a South African diamond magnate who acquired the estate in 1903 and remodelled the house as a setting for his outstanding art collection while retaining Capability Brown's great park with its twin lakes. In addition to the Luton Hoo pictures there are ivories, enamels and Renaissance jewels and metalwork. Sir Harold favoured English furniture and purchased many fine examples while his mother, Lady

Ludlow, built a collection of 18th century English porcelain. To these treasures Lady Zia added her own unique display of Imperial Russian objects including examples by Fabergé. Lady Zia was the daughter of His Imperial Highness Grand Duke Michael of Russia and the Countess de Torby. She and Sir Harold, who attained the rank of Major-General during World War II and was chairman of the giant Electrolux group of companies for nearly 40 years, married in 1917. Sir Harold died in 1973 and his wife four years later.

The Wernher family could be regarded as lucky owners. In addition to their four Classic successes with Meld and Charlottown, their green and yellow quartered colours were carried with great distinction by that versatile stayer Brown Jack and the talented middle-distance colt Aggressor.

Sir Harold, an enthusiastic man to hounds, bought Brown Jack when he was Master of the Fernie, primarily as a jumper. Brown Jack cost £750 plus a further £50 contingency fee if he ever won a race. The remarkable Irish-bred gelding in fact won seven of his ten jumping events – including the 1928 Champion Hurdle at Cheltenham – and 18 of his 55 starts on the Flat! He developed into one of the most celebrated stayers in English racing history and certainly the most popular of the between-the-wars period.

Brown Jack's greatest claim to lasting fame was his unique series of victories in the two-mile-six-furlong Queen Alexandra Stakes at Royal Ascot. Ridden by the equally popular Steve Donoghue, Brown Jack carried off this race six years in succession. His final Queen Alexandra triumph, achieved in 1934 when he was a 10-year-old, produced unforgettable scenes of admiration and affection but the old horse's trainer, Ivor Anthony, could not bring himself to watch.

Legend has it that Anthony sat under a tree in the paddock until the ringing cheers made it evident that Brown Jack, that standing Ascot dish, had won yet again. But Brown Jack was not merely an Ascot specialist. During his extraordinary career he carried off the Goodwood, Doncaster and Chester Cups and won the Ebor Handicap at York with 9st 5lb in the plate. That particular weight-carrying record stood until another great

121

Champion Hurdler, Sea Pigeon, humped 9st 10lb to victory in 1979.

Brown Jack, foaled in 1924, lived in cosseted retirement at his owners' home until his death in 1948. Seven years later the Wernhers bred Aggressor, a bay horse by the Sussex Stakes winner Combat out of the Nearco mare Phaetonia. But Sir Harold and Lady Zia came within 250 guineas of selling this fine colt as a yearling. Cecil Boyd-Rochfort, on a visit to the Blackhall Stud in County Kildare, where the Someries foals were kept after being weaned from their dams, decided that Aggressor was below standard and advised Sir Harold to send him to the Ballsbridge Sales in Dublin without a reserve.

Only at the last moment did the naturally cautious Sir Harold amend this plan by insisting on a modest 1,000 guinea reserve being put on the ugly duckling youngster. Happily for his breeder, the bidding for Aggressor stopped at 750 guineas and he was led out of the Ballsbridge ring unsold. As Boyd-Rochfort was still not interested in having Aggressor as a member of his highly-select string, Sir Harold sent the reject to Jack Gosden at Lewes in the hope that he might develop into a decent handicapper.

Aggressor never became a swan but what he lacked in physical attraction he more than made up for by displaying a high degree of courage and ability, winning 11 races to a value of more than £36,000, a sum equivalent to perhaps £200,000 at today's prize-money levels.

Most notable of his successes was Aggressor's defeat of that brilliant filly Petite Etoile in the 1960 King George VI and Queen Elizabeth Stakes. Although Jimmy Lindley rode Aggressor that day at Ascot, Scobie Breasley played a telling part in determining the outcome of the 'King George' and in helping to bring about the downfall of Petite Etoile and her jockey Lester Piggott.

The story behind that controversial race is one of intrigue and revenge. Had Dick Francis written it as a sub-plot in one of his hugely successful racing thrillers he would have been accused of over-dramatizing. The Breasley-inspired plot to beat Piggott in the 1960 'King George' will be told in the next chapter,

122

but how strange the linking thread in racing can be. 'Towser' Gosden, Jimmy Lindley, Gordon Smyth, the Wernhers and Breasley himself all connect via such horses as Aggressor and Charlottown.

Lindley's part in the saga comes back into sharp focus during the 1966 season as, after Charlottown's defeat by Epsom fourth Sodium in the Irish Sweeps Derby, Scobie Breasley was injured and Sir Harold Wernher turned once more to Lindley to ride his horse in the St Leger.

However, the Irish Derby merits careful analysis first. Breasley has been blamed for the fact that Sodium was able to turn the Epsom form inside-out at the Curragh less than a month later. Such criticism appears unfounded viewed with the benefit of hindsight. Sodium, a later-maturing colt, was probably Charlottown's superior on his best form but, unfortunately for punters, lacked consistency. Charlottown started 11-8 on in Ireland but Sodium, never a real threat in the Epsom Derby, beat him by a length, and quite a comfortable length at that. Scobie's detractors were up in arms, accusing the Australian of giving Charlottown too much ground to make up. But this argument simply does not hold water. 'We were no further back at the Curragh than we were at Epsom', Breasley insists. And his view is readily supported by Sodium's rider, Frank Durr, now a successful trainer. 'Scobie and I kicked on at an almost identical point but my horse was just the better that particular day', Durr asserts.

An independent assessment from *Timeform's Racehorses of 1966* serves to underline that Breasley's judgement was not at fault. Their well-argued findings are: 'It is true that Charlottown came from a long way behind but so did Sodium and the one was not very far behind the other turning into the straight. Both made their challenge at almost the same time. Charlottown had to come on the outside but the result did not seem affected. Charlottown had every chance of winning from the two-furlong marker but although he made steady progress throughout the last furlong, Sodium always had the edge.'

The views of George Todd, Sodium's gifted trainer, are also highly pertinent. Todd, who trained on the splendid Manton

123

Downs above Marlborough, had held a licence since 1928 and was a man of patience and wide-ranging experience. Yet even he found Sodium something of a puzzle. Todd had expected his colt to very nearly win at Epsom and he was mystified that Sodium weakened in the final stages of the Derby just at the moment when his trainer had anticipated he would be running on to take a hand in the finish. Right up until his death at the age of 84 in 1974, George Todd insisted that for some reason Sodium failed to show his best form at Epsom. That being so, Sodium had reasonable expectations for the Sweeps Derby and almost certainly won it strictly on merit.

But the Charlottown-Sodium story was not yet at an end. After the latter had been beaten by Aunt Edith in the King George VI and Queen Elizabeth Stakes, the two Derby winners were back on a collision course for the St Leger. But first they were scheduled to meet in the Oxfordshire Stakes at Newbury with opinions sharply divided as to which would emerge superior this time round.

The Oxfordshire Stakes took place on what proved to be one of Sodium's unco-operative afternoons. Perhaps his biorhythms were out of sequence. More likely, he was simply a horse with two ideas of the merits of strenuous physical exercise. Whatever the reason, Newbury racegoers needed telescopes to find him as Sodium ran a wretchedly poor race to finish well behind Charlottown, who beat a decent animal named Desert Call II by five lengths.

This result looked an obvious pointer to the probable outcome of the St Leger and Scobie Breasley, gradually recovering from his injuries, intensified his efforts to be race-riding fit in time for Doncaster's final Classic of the season. In fact, he failed to pass the doctor but, in any case, yet another twist in the Charlottown-Sodium saga was on the cards. Not surprisingly, Charlottown started Leger favourite and ran his usual game and reliable race. But Sodium, that self-willed horse, had obviously decided it was time to level the series and got up close home to master his old rival by a neck.

Lindley held up Charlottown behind the leaders and did not attempt to improve his mount's position until after turning into

124

*Drinks all round as Scobie celebrates his 2,000th winner in England, Fair
Chantress, at Windsor in August 1966.*

Doncaster's long and unrelenting home straight. The Derby winner looked to be going well enough when brought to challenge David Jack three furlongs out but it took Charlottown more than a quarter of a mile to shake off that colt and he had nothing in reserve to withstand the late challenge of Sodium.

But even after the photo-finish verdict had confirmed Sodium's narrow victory, Charlottown supporters were hopeful of collecting. It was not necessary to be an expert race-reader to see that the two leading contenders had come very close together in the final 100 yards and many people held the view that they had actually touched and that Sodium was the culprit of this discernible interference. The Doncaster Stewards thought otherwise and allowed the placing to remain unchanged to the obvious delight of Sodium's owner, Radha Sigtia, a silk merchant from Bombay.

Mr Sigtia declined to run Sodium in the Prix de l'Arc de Triomphe, a race for which Charlottown was never entered. But both colts were kept in training as four-year-olds. Charlottown, having been somewhat controversially voted Racehorse of the Year for 1966, underlined the virtue of that award by proving himself better than Sodium in 1967.

In fact, Gordon Smyth's colt carried off both the John Porter Stakes at Newbury and Epsom's Coronation Cup. In the latter race not only was he able to beat Sodium again but also to lower the colours of Nelcius, the previous year's French Derby winner. It was then decided to take him campaigning in France and he was aimed at the competitive Grand Prix de Saint-Cloud. Unhappily, Charlottown ran the only poor race of his career on the Paris track, finishing sixth of eight starters, and was retired. Equally sadly, he failed to establish a worthwhile reputation as a stallion and was eventually exported to Australia.

Sodium deteriorated at four and failed to win from six starts. He was then sold to stand in France for a figure never made public but believed to be in the region of £100,000. Since Sodium's three victories had earned prize-money of more than £96,000 he was quite a money-spinner for Radha Sigtia, who had given only 3,500 guineas for the son of 1961 Derby winner Psidium as a yearling.

126

He was always a more impressive specimen than Charlottown from the point of view of physique but the narrow, somewhat greyhound conformation of the 1966 Derby winner should not detract from the fact that Charlottown was possessed of a notably fine action and that his small frame contained a large amount of courage. Naturally enough, Scobie was very fond of him and says of the horse who provided his second Derby triumph: 'A really nice little horse. He may not have been absolutely top-class but he showed himself to be tough, game and adaptable on Derby Day and that was good enough. I think he was a kinder horse than Sodium although the results show them to have had just about the same ability.'

Overleaf: *Old Tom (second from right) wins the 38-runner Lincoln Handicap at Doncaster in 1965. Scobie rode Riot Act to land this event again the following year when there were 49 starters.*

127

14

Lester...the Admirable Enemy

'Of all my rivals – either in Australia or in England – Lester
Piggott was the hardest man to beat.' Scobie Breasley makes
that short statement with a degree of feeling, a combination of
admiration and indignation. The series of epic battles between
the experienced, canny Australian and his younger but equally
gifted and more explosive English opponent brought a bite
to the British racing scene throughout the early 1960s. Their
rivalry was always fierce, occasionally ferocious and constantly
entertaining.

It would be quite wrong to depict Breasley and Piggott as
disliking each other. Actually, each holds the other in respect
but their feud to settle which could claim supremacy as England's
leading rider, fuelled by an extraordinary level of Press coverage,
was real enough. Neither asked nor gave any quarter and the
intensity of their many clashes had the effect of splitting the
sporting public into sharply-divided factions. Nor was this
limited to everyday followers of horse racing. Breasley fans eyed
Piggott supporters with thinly-disguised contempt across the
normally decorous lawns of English racecourses. Piggott buffs
glared back. The nation was divided. This, after all, was not
David versus Goliath but rather Goliath versus Goliath since
both jockeys, men of exceptional ability, were established racing
giants.

Although these two had been competing one with the other
on a daily basis since Scobie's arrival from Australia ten years
before, it was in 1960 that battle lines were really drawn. Lester
was champion that year with 170 winners, 17 more than Scobie.
But the following season the positions were reversed, Breasley
finishing with a total of 171, just seven more than his rival. A
lengthy suspension effectively wrecked the Piggott 1962 chal-

lenge – more of that shortly – and Breasley was a runaway winner with his highest seasonal total of 179 winners.

But the 1963 title race went to the Australian in a photo-finish, just a single winner separating them at 176 to 175. Bookmakers claim to have laid more bets on the jockeys' championship that year than they did on the outcome of the Derby. Newspapers published the respective scores in banner headlines every day as the season drew towards its climax, the great race news spilling off the sports pages on to the front of even the 'serious' journals. No racing story had been more widely covered before and certainly none has since.

Fleet Street sports editors issued standing instructions to their racing correspondents to concentrate all their attention on the epic title-race battle and both jockeys were constantly pestered to state their respective views on the outcome of the championship. This was a game which both Scobie Breasley and Lester Piggott found tiresome in the extreme, each preferring to be left alone in order to devote himself fully to the task of finishing the season in front.

'Of course, it was flattering that the whole country seemed caught up in my struggle against Lester, but the Press boys hardly gave us a moment', Scobie says. 'All the attention was on Breasley v. Piggott and every day the pressure grew. So did the misquotes in the newspapers. I've never liked people crediting me with things I didn't say but a lot of it went on during the 1963 season. I'm sure Lester suffered in much the same way.'

There is no doubt that certain reporters tried to build up a level of personal emnity between the two men which never really existed. The long-drawn-out title race was good copy made even more sensational by the implication that Breasley and Piggott were at daggers drawn. They were not, but it is true to say that they were not bosom pals either.

Fuel was added to the fire by the complete contrast in personality and riding styles, not to mention the generation gap between these supremely talented protagonists. After all, Scobie, at 49, was already a veteran in terms of professional race-riding while his great rival was still two years short of his 30th birthday, and Breasley's quiet and thoughtful method could hardly have less resembled that of the hard-riding and flamboyant Piggott.

The advantage seesawed first one way and then the other, sometimes even a single winner tipping the advantage in favour of one jockey only for the next meeting to redress the balance. Some punters were even prepared to take odds about a title dead-heat, although only one such result had been recorded this century in British Flat racing when Steve Donoghue and Charlie Elliott shared the 1923 championship with 89 winners each.

A contemporary – and expert – view of the keen rivalry between these master jockeys is offered by another fine Australian rider, Edgar Britt, in his book *Post Haste* (published in 1967 by Frederick Muller Ltd). Britt, having ridden his first winner as a 16-year-old in 1930, had a 30-year career in the saddle and knew Scobie Breasley's style and tactics better than most. He rated Breasley alongside Jim Pike as the greatest jockey produced by Australia during that era. Britt wrote: 'Those two great rivals Lester Piggott and Scobie Breasley provided the fire and the ice of British racing, Piggott a dashing rider, prepared to take a risk and Breasley the coolest jockey against whom I ever rode. Piggott and Breasley had one attribute in common and from it stemmed their consistent battle each season to finish as leading jockey – each rode as keenly in every race as though he were in the early days of his apprenticeship.'

Occasionally, according to Edgar Britt, that keenness over-stepped the bounds of fair competition. Britt believes these was a time when the Breasley-Piggott rivalry came close to develop-ing into the greatest feud in racing history when they were both striving to take over the mantle vacated by Gordon Richards. He catalogues several races in which the battle almost developed into a full-scale war, notably a race at Sandown Park in which Scobie had drawn the rails with Lester number three at the gate and Britt between them.

'I could tell that Lester was trying to beat the start and go in on top of Scobie who, wise in the ways of racing, knew this and was just as anxious to start well and move out. I was going to be the ham in the sandwich so told them "Do your feuding when I'm not around". While Scobie and Lester remained great

Head-to-head. Scobie and Lester Piggott clash during their 1961 championship battle. Scobie took the title that year.

rivals, the heat of those days faded. There was plenty of room at the top for them both. Despite the difference in their ages, there was very little difference in ability between them. Scobie was never a dirty rider but he loved the rails. Australian sport has had no finer ambassador than Scobie Breasley.'

That is a view almost universally shared by British racegoers who still remember Scobie's unique skills and hold him in the warm affection normally reserved for one of their own.

Breasley himself, while adamant that on no occasion during his long career in the saddle did he ever deliberately put the safety of a fellow jockey at risk, admits that some of his rides against Lester Piggott were hard, give-and-take affairs. 'Lester and I had a right go back in 1960 which nearly ended in a punch-up', Scobie recalls. 'A whole series of incidents got my back up and I was very upset at some of Lester's antics.

133

I remember riding in the Midlands one day that season – Wolverhampton I think it was – when Piggott cut up my mount for no reason at all. He was going to win the race anyway but he seemed to want to put me over the rails. It made my blood boil.

'My first reaction was to give Lester a smack on the nose but the only way to get back at him that made any sense was to hit him where it would hurt most – in the pocket. Getting involved in a fight could have cost me my licence so I would have finished worse off.

'The grey filly Petite Etoile was *the* horse of the moment. She had won the previous season's 1,000 Guineas and Oaks and in 1960 had landed the Coronation Cup. She was going to be a real hot-shot for the King George VI and Queen Elizabeth Stakes at Ascot with Lester on her back. That would be the day to teach Lester a lesson.

'My mount, the Irish colt Sunny Court, had no real chance of winning but I decided to do my level best to stop Lester collecting the big prize. I didn't intend to break the rules but I was determined to give Lester a hard time and so square the books. It worked a treat.

'By the time Lester had shaken me off and got out of the pocket on the rails Jimmy Lindley and Aggressor had the race won. Petite Etoile, 5-2 on, was beaten half a length. I was only sixth but came back grinning like a Cheshire cat. Everyone thought that Lester had ridden a bad race and Jimmy Lindley probably thinks to this day that he and Aggressor stole the King George but that's the real story of how the wonder-filly was beaten, although I've never revealed how I got my own back before. In normal circumstances I would have given Lester plenty of room if his mount was going so much better than mine, but this time I kept the door firmly shut. Of course, Lester knew perfectly well what had gone on but, to give him his due, he didn't complain. In fact, he never said a word to anyone about prevented his filly getting a decent run.

'There was no inquiry by the Stewards and Lester, asked by the Press how the "unbeatable" Petite Etoile had failed to win, made one of his most priceless remarks. "I think they cut the grass the wrong way", he said.

134

'Lester took it like a man. He's never mentioned it from that day to this – at least not to me – but he never tried to put me over the rails again.'

Geoff Lewis, a close friend of Scobie and his family, also rode in that King George, gaining a place on the giant Kythnos. Later he was to become stable jockey to Petite Etoile's trainer, Noel Murless. He reached the pinnacle of his riding career in 1971 when winning the Derby and the Prix de l'Arc de Triomphe on Mill Reef, one of the greatest post-war champions of European racing and now a highly successful National Stud stallion. Lewis retired from the saddle in 1979 and followed Scobie's example by becoming an Epsom trainer. He has quickly established himself in this new role, and last year saddled Yawa to win the Grand Prix de Paris at Longchamp, the scene of his triumphant Arc victory with Mill Reef 12 years earlier.

Meanwhile, Lester Piggott rides on . . . and on. Now a veteran himself, Lester has won virtually every worthwhile race in Europe and many major events further afield but two ambitions remain. He would dearly love to bring his tally of Derby victories to 10 – he needs only one more to achieve that aim – and to top Frank Buckle's record of 27 English Classic wins. Two more are required in order to clinch that achievement. 'I wouldn't mind a small bet that Lester does both before he hangs up his saddle', remarks Scobie. 'He is a tremendous jockey and a dedicated professional. Only Sir Gordon stands above him in my estimation and there's never going to be another like him.'

But Scobie's cool and complimentary assessment of Piggott's outstanding career is made easier now that the Australian is no longer involved at the 'sharp end' of racing. When both men were on collision course with the championship their common goal, Breasley was less free with his praise and Piggott equally tight-lipped on the subject of his Australian opponent. 'I didn't spend much time talking about Lester in those days and I doubt if he was very keen to talk about me.'

Overleaf: *Has anyone seen the horses? Scobie and his great rival Lester Piggott pictured at Epsom in 1964.*

136

In 1961, the first of those neck-and-neck title races, the championship remained undecided until the final few days of the season. With a month to go, Lester held a narrow advantage, reaching the 150-winner mark three ahead of Scobie. But Piggott fell from his throne, quite literally, in a dramatic crash at Lingfield Park on the penultimate day of the term. Scobie was already a nose in front and took full advantage of Lester's fall, and of the resultant shaking which caused him to stand down for the remainder of the day, by landing a treble. The big race was won and lost with Scobie regaining the crown after a four-year gap.

Battle lines were drawn up again for 1962 but the great confrontation failed to materialize, much to the regret of a fascinated public. Piggott suffered a lengthy riding ban handed out by the Stewards of the Jockey Club. That suspension still remains a highly contentious matter more than 20 years later. Riding a horse named Ione in a selling plate at the now defunct Lincoln course in the May of that year, Piggott finished two lengths behind that horse's stable companion Polly Macaw, partnered by the late Peter Robinson. Both horses were trained by Bob Ward. The local Stewards held an inquiry into Piggott's riding and decided to suspend him for the remainder of the meeting and report the case to the Jockey Club.

Lester Piggott was called before the Jockey Club five days later and following his appearance a sparsely-worded statement was published in the Racing Calendar which said: 'After hearing further evidence the Stewards of the Jockey Club considered that L. Piggott, the rider of Ione, had made no effort to win the race and withdrew his licence to ride from today's date until July 28, inclusive. The Stewards further informed R. Ward, the trainer of Ione and Polly Macaw, that they considered those two horses had not been allowed to run on their merits. They were satisfied beyond all reasonable doubt that Ward was a party to this infringement of the Rules and they withdrew his licence to train.'

So, in a few carefully-chosen words, Lester's involvement in the 1962 jockeys' title was ended. He rode fewer than 100 winners that year and finished only fourth in the list behind

Scobie, previous champion Doug Smith and Ron Hutchinson.

Breasley's winning tally of 179 was the highest seasonal total he achieved and included four four-timers, 15 trebles and 30 doubles. Incidentally, Scobie recorded one five-timer during his spell in England. He achieved this rare feat at Lewes – a course over which he excelled – in August 1960. Those five wins came in consecutive races but he was beaten into third place on his final ride of the afternoon. Evidently, the Sussex air suited him since Scobie partnered a total of 201 winners at nearby Brighton and also had a commendable record at Goodwood.

But if, from the point of view of close competition, 1962 was something of an anti-climax, the following year was a sensation. Back and forth went the lead as Breasley and Piggott travelled the country in pursuit of winners. First one was favourite and then the other but when the last race of the season had been decided, when the last bet had been settled it was the Australian who was champion for the third time in succession. Scobie Breasley, rising 50 years of age, had once again defied the passage of time to keep up with a younger rival and then, by a supreme effort, pip him to the post.

15

The Great Jockeys

The between-the-wars period is often called, in both Australia and England, the Golden Age of jockeyship. Standards were high, competition fierce and, because money was harder to come by, racing produced 'hungry' riders in much the same way that boxing, during the same era, profited from 'hungry' fighters. There were few hand-outs from benevolent and caring welfare states in the 1920s and '30s. 'Times were tough when I started out' recalls Scobie. 'You needed to make your own way in racing and in the world in general. If you had the ability – and the luck – the rewards were there to be enjoyed, but people were not inclined to stand back and let someone else have the first shot.

'It's still difficult to reach the top as a jockey. You only need look back at the list of those who were promising apprentices a few years ago and work out how many really made it. The number is small, depressingly small. For every kid who starts off with high hopes and rides a few winners to think he's on his way to fame and fortune is just a painful illusion. Only a handful get there for the simple reason that room at the top is very scarce. But if you're good enough and lucky enough it's a wonderful life as a professional jockey.'

Scobie Breasley's lengthy career in the saddle, combined with his worldwide experience, makes him exceptionally, if not uniquely, qualified to judge the merits of the other great jockeys of his time, a period spanning 40 years.

When Scobie was a tiny apprentice, Bobby Lewis was his hero. Then came Jim Pike, an unfamiliar name to British race-goers but, according to Breasley and many other fine judges of horsemanship, one of the really outstanding Australian riders. Scobie's eyes still light up when he speaks of Pike's skills in the saddle. 'He was a rider of the very highest international class, one of the true greats', says Scobie with a degree of certainty which leaves no room for argument. 'Jimmy didn't like to travel very much. He wouldn't even go to America with Phar Lap. That was a pity, because if he had, he would have been known and respected throughout the world and not just in Australia.

'You must remember that he was the top man when there were so many good riders at home. He was up against real opposition, great jockeys in their own right like Jim and Darby Munro, Billy Cook, Frank Dempsey, Hughie Cairns, Maurice McCarten, Keith Voitre, Neville Percival and half a dozen others. Billy Duncan was another. Any of those fellows would give a horse a top-class ride so for Pike to be the pick – and he was in my book at least – means he was a champion among champions.'

Scobie makes no attempt at direct comparison between riders of different generations, holding the view that the only fair method is to compare like with like. 'It's difficult, perhaps impossible, to look at a jockey who rode 50 years ago and decide he was better or worse than one riding now. You can't do that any more than you can state that Lester Piggott is greater or less great than Fred Archer. But you can judge a rider alongside those he rode against or those he is riding against today. That's why I feel certain that Jim Pike, for example, was a brilliant jockey as he was up against so many other fine riders.

'The same can be said about Sir Gordon Richards. He was riding at a time when overall standards were very high in England, your own Golden Age. Gordon was nearly at the end of his career when he and I were rivals but he was still absolutely outstanding. When people press me to name the best jockey I ever saw I must put Sir Gordon first. But Jim Pike and Lester Piggott obviously get close.

'Another great Australian was Rae Johnstone and European racing fans know all about him. Rae and I had several things in common. We both came from New South Wales, both did well as youngsters back home but both really made it big when we left Australia for Europe. Of course, Rae came over a long time before me, in 1932 to be exact. But he went to France where they called him "Le Crocodile" because he liked to snap up his

141

rivals from behind – another similarity! He was a big-race specialist and won every French and English Classic and a couple of Arc de Triomphes. A wonderful record. But that doesn't mean to say that he just coasted along in other races. After all, he was champion jockey of France three times in his first six years there. He was a fine judge of pace and a splendid tactical rider. He was also quite a stylist which you can't say of all Australian jockeys.'

'But Rae had his bad times, too. He had a short spell in England before World War II, but was upset by some pretty harsh words when he got beaten on the Guineas winner Colombo in the 1934 Derby, and cleared off back to France. He must have wished he had stayed put later on when the Germans shoved him into a prison camp. That was rough on Rae but he came through the war and was better than ever afterwards.'

William Raphael Johnstone, to give him his imposing full name, was nine years Scobie's senior. He rode his first winner at the age of 15 and was champion jockey in Sydney just a decade later. He first went to France at the invitation of Pierre Wertheimer, a leading figure on the Turf there for more than 50 years and a successful and influential owner. Johnstone won the 1935 1,000 Guineas in his famous blue and white colours, riding Mesa. She was slightly difficult to settle but was still heavily backed to land the Oaks, only for Johnstone to ride what is widely thought of as being a very indifferent race. In fact, like many good jockeys both before and since, Johnstone appeared to have problems with the tricky Epsom track but he conquered it in the end, returning after the war to win the Derby on My Love (1948), Galcador (1950) and Lavandin (1956). He was also successful in the Oaks on three occasions with Imprudence (1947), Asmena (1950) and Sun Cap (1954).

Rae Johnstone retired from the saddle in 1957 to set up as a trainer at Chantilly. He had a good measure of success but died shortly after suffering a heart attack while racing at Le Tremblay in 1964. 'That was a very sad day for the Australian racing community' says Scobie. 'Rae was such a bright and charming man, good company always. He made his home in France, spoke the language well and was always helpful to fellow jockeys

142

A fistful of Aussie riding talent. From the left: Garnie Bougoure, George Moore, Scobie Breasley, Ron Hutchinson and Bill Williamson.

who could not. I was very fond of him and admired him, too.'

Johnstone's European trail-blazing undoubtedly made things easier for those of his fellow-countrymen who followed his example. He alerted owners, trainers and other Turf professionals to the fact that Australia was producing talented jockeys who could more than hold their own in this part of the world, and the exodus of Aussie jockeys to try their luck in Europe soon swelled to a near flood. Among the top-flight men, apart from Edgar Britt, Johnstone and Scobie Breasley himself, were Ron Hutchinson, George Moore and Bill Williamson.

Ron Hutchinson is 13 years younger than Scobie and by the time he won his first race on a horse named Busybody at Mentone in Victoria in 1943, the second year of his apprenticeship with C. A. Goodfellow, Breasley was already a well-established jockey. But the age gap has not prevented these two Australians, near neighbours in England, from becoming close friends. 'The Little Man and I are great buddies' says Scobie. 'We spend countless hours arguing about everything under the sun! When Ron and his wife, Norma, come over for dinner or May and I go to visit them it's like an all-Australian debating society.

Of course, I'm nearly always right but that doesn't worry Ron, he'll go right on telling me I'm wrong until the early hours of the morning.'

Hutchinson, frequently nicknamed 'Bobber' by English racing fans because of his unique movement, apparently out of sequence with the stride-pattern of the horses he rode, enjoyed a profitable period of nearly 20 years riding in England, having arrived here via the Irish stable of Paddy Prendergast in the early 1960s. His first important ride in this country was on the Prendergast-trained Martial in the 2,000 Guineas of 1960. To the dismay of favourite backers, Hutchinson got Martial up close home to beat hot-pot Venture VII, ridden by George Moore who was then based in France. Martial started at odds of 18-1, Venture VII was a 6-4 chance. But if the majority of punters at Newmarket that day looked at the new Australian import somewhat balefully as they counted their losses, the British racing public at large soon took a liking to the sandy-haired Hutchinson and within a few years he had established a faithful following almost the size of Scobie's.

Paddy Prendergast was then at the height of his powers as a trainer – he won the English championship three times during the 1960s – and Ron Hutchinson rode this wave for all he was worth, gaining his first Royal Ascot success on Typhoon in the Coventry Stakes of 1960. The following year saw him win such important events as the National Stakes and the Cheveley Park Stakes on that fast filly Display, the Nunthorpe Stakes (now re-titled the William Hill Sprint Championship) on Floribunda and the Champagne Stakes on Clear Sound. When the Prendergast-Hutchinson partnership came to an end, Ron settled in England and began to ride for the late Duke of Norfolk's then private stable at Arundel and for Harry Wragg and Sir Jack Jarvis at Newmarket. It was Wragg, a great jockey in his day, who provided 'Bobber' Hutchinson with two further Classic winners, Full Dress II and Intermezzo in the 1,000 Guineas and St Leger of 1969. But Hutchinson was never to win a Derby. How he came to lose the mount on 1966 Epsom hero Charlottown to Scobie has already been told, but he also lost out on Shirley Heights, the 1978 winner.

By 1977, the Castle yard at Arundel had 'gone public' with John Dunlop training a string more than 100-strong there and Ron, although now a veteran, was still the first jockey. But he was being troubled by an injured hip joint and considering retirement. He decided, halfway through the season, that it was to be his last as a jockey in England although, as it happened, he rode the Singapore and Peninsula circuit for a couple of years afterwards with great success. Had the popular little Australian realised that Shirley Heights, whom he rode as a two-year-old that season, would win the following year's Derby and Irish Sweeps Derby he would, no doubt, have delayed his journey to the Far East a little longer. 'I knew Shirley Heights was a decent colt but he was never very sound', Ron Hutchinson said later. 'It was not even certain that he would stand training as a three-year-old.' He was very nearly right in that respect, for soon after landing his Derby double, Shirley Heights did in fact break down and was retired to stud.

Greville Starkey was the man chosen to replace Hutchinson as partner for Shirley Heights and he is, I feel sure, conscious of the fact that Shirley Heights owed his big-race victories, in part at least, to Ron Hutchinson's restrained and considerate handling of the colt as a juvenile. Riding quality horses with not only that day's race but the next outing in mind was always one of 'Bobber' Hutchinson's great strengths. 'Ron was a very sympathetic jockey and a very good one', affirms Scobie. 'But I'm not sure we should say so – it gives him and me one less topic to argue about.'

Ron Hutchinson underwent a hip operation on his return to England from Singapore. Thankfully it was completely success-ful and he continues to lead an active life among horses, having converted some boxes and built others to take animals out-of-training at his Surrey home, where he also has an equine swim-ming pool. His son Raymond, a vet, is a top-class amateur rider.

George Moore, currently the champion trainer in Hong Kong, was one of Australian racing's most accomplished jockeys both at home and overseas in a riding career which lasted from 1940 to 1971. 'George was top-class, a very clever jockey' says Scobie. 'He won most things worth winning but oddly enough, just like me, he never managed to get his hands on the Melbourne Cup.' Moore's first victory was on New Year's Day, 1940, in Brisbane. That win heralded a notable professional life but it was not until 1959 that the racing fraternity outside Australia came to realise the prowess he commanded. That was the date of his arrival in France to ride for Alec Head's powerful Chantilly stable whose principal patron was the flamboyant Aly Khan. George Moore made an immediate impression on both sides of the Channel, an impression he was to consolidate eight years later.

In France he landed the Prix de l'Arc de Triomphe on Saint Crespin III; in England the 2,000 Guineas on Taboun. The following year he took France by storm, adding both the Prix du Jockey-Club (French Derby) and the Grand Prix de Paris to his haul on Charlottesville, sire of Scobie Breasley's 1966 Epsom Derby-winning mount, Charlottown. Despite that narrow defeat in the 2,000 Guineas of 1960, Moore also plundered the big races in England, winning the Ascot Gold Cup on Sheshoon and both the St James's Palace Stakes and the Sussex Stakes on Guineas runner-up Venture VII. Yet he returned to Australia at the end of the season, Aly Khan having been killed in a car crash during the year.

It is sometimes overlooked that he made a fleeting visit to England in 1961, flying all the way from Australia to ride Sovrango in the Derby. Sovrango, trained by Harry Wragg, was very strongly fancied but could finish only fourth to his stable-mate Psidium (Roger Poincelet) who started at 66-1, the longest odds recorded for a Derby winner during the post-war period. George Moore must have wondered if his journey had been really necessary. But there were no such doubts about his ride in the 1967 running of the great Epsom Classic. Noel Murless had asked the Australian back as contract jockey to the Warren Place stable, seeking a man of proven ability to take over from Lester Piggott, who had turned freelance after a long association with the leading Newmarket yard.

The 1967 season was nothing short of a sensational triumph for the Murless-Moore partnership. Together they carried off three Classics – the 2,000 Guineas and Derby with Mr Jim Joel's Royal Palace and the 1,000 Guineas with Fleet, the property of

Kent fruit-farmer and hop-grower Robert Boucher. But those major wins by no means tell the full story of an exceptional year for Warren Place. Busted landed the King George VI and Queen Elizabeth Stakes at Ascot, Pink Gem dead-heated for the Park Hill Stakes, the Queen's Hopeful Venture carried off the Princess of Wales Stakes while Sun Rock (Gordon Stakes) and Sucaryl (Extel Handicap) scored at Goodwood. These exploits resulted in Murless becoming the first English trainer to win for his patrons more than a quarter of a million pounds in a single season, Royal Palace contributing nearly £93,000 to a magnificent total figure of £256,899. That prize-money record stood until 1975 despite the slipping value of the pound as inflation rocked European currencies.

George Moore, even allowing for the fact that he was riding for the most powerful stable in the land and taking the mounts on carefully-selected horses, enjoyed a season of almost unbroken glory. He rode 72 winners from only 233 mounts, a success rate of more than 30 per cent. Backers soon caught on, supporting Moore's mounts blindly. They rarely left the racecourse empty-handed. But not all sections of British racing shared the punters' delight and some individual, or group of malcontents, decided to scare off the Australian jockey. His London flat was broken into and vandalized. Even clothes hanging in the wardrobe there were slashed to pieces.

The message was all too clear – leave England or suffer some very nasty consequences. This disgraceful harassment, sad to say, succeeded in frightening Moore who quit England, never to return. The best efforts of the police failed to find the culprits and, to this day, one can only speculate about who might have been responsible. The implied threat to George Moore was the most unsavoury chapter in British racing since the notorious razor gangs of the 1930s. 'It was a crying shame that George was treated in such a fashion and somehow all the more so because it came at the end of a season during which he had carried all before him', says Scobie Breasley. 'I thought those sort of tricks were a thing of the past but George was frightened and no one could blame him for that.'

Racing had exhibited its least acceptable facet. Any business

The Australian connection. Scobie poses with his great pal Bill Williamson.

in which huge sums of money change hands on a daily basis tends to attract a criminal element, and it would be foolish to pretend otherwise. But the largely respectable British Turf community felt shamed that a guest in this country should have been so scandalously treated.

George Moore retired from the saddle in 1971 at the comparatively early age of 48, but his son Gary maintained the family tradition of riding big-race winners when he flew in from Hong Kong to land the 1981 Prix de l'Arc de Triomphe on Gold River, a filly trained by Alec Head. It was Head who had saddled Saint Crespin III to win the Arc with George Moore in the plate precisely 22 years earlier. Alec Head, whose son Freddie had turned down the ride on Gold River in order to partner the 1980 winner, Detroit, greeted Gary Moore in the Longchamp winners' enclosure with the words: 'This makes me feel old'.

Bill Williamson (1922-1979) was, at least in one respect, the odd-man-out among the top Australians who furthered their riding careers in the Northern Hemisphere. Although a brilliant judge of pace, even by the standards of a Breasley or a Johnstone, he preferred to pull his mounts towards the outside of the field in the home straight and bring his horses with a single, uninterrupted run well clear of any potential hazard. Greatly respected by his fellow jockeys, Williamson was once described by no less an authority than Lester Piggott as 'the greatest big-race rider in the world'. Scobie, while not going to such extremes, was a Williamson fan, too. He says: 'If I was ice-cool, Bill was deep-frozen. You would never see him in a flap and he was undoubtedly one of the very best Australians to come to Europe. He also happened to be a very nice man.'

Known as 'Weary Willie' because of his heavy-lidded eyes and a constantly lugubrious facial expression, Williamson did not leave Australia until 1960 when he was already 38 years of age. He had been riding winners in his native country since 1937, but because his personality reflected his shyness and reticence and his horsemanship was equally low-key, his international reputation had been slow to build. However, Williamson soon prospered in this part of the world and his riding services were greatly in demand in England, Ireland and France. He partnered only two English Classic winners, Abermaid (1962) and Night Off (1965) in the 1,000 Guineas, but had ten such successes in Ireland. One of the highlights of his career was his 1972 Irish Sweeps Derby victory on Steel Pulse, a colt trained by his friend Scobie Breasley.

Many people believe that Williamson should have won the 1972 Epsom Derby, too, but his admirer Lester Piggott came in for the mount on Roberto that year due to rather unfortunate circumstances – at least, unfortunate from an Australian point of view. Williamson had ridden Roberto into second place

149

behind High Top (Willie Carson) in the 2,000 Guineas at New-market. It was fully expected, not least by Williamson himself, that he would have the mount again on this Vincent O'Brien-trained colt in the premier Classic. But matters conspired against him. Soon after the Guineas, Williamson took a heavy fall when riding at Kempton Park and even though his own doctor had passed him fit to resume by Derby week, trainer O'Brien and Roberto's American owner, John Galbreath, decided to replace him with Piggott. They apparently held lingering doubts that Bill Williamson had made a full recovery, but the decision to substitute him was hard-headed and unpopular with the English racing public despite the assurance that Williamson would receive his full win percentage should Roberto finish in first place. As things worked out, Roberto's connections made absolutely the right choice of Derby rider if not, perhaps, for the right reasons.

Even discounting any after-effects of Williamson's injuries or his lack of race practice, he simply did not possess Piggott's strength in the finish, and it was this characteristic which carried the day in Roberto's tremendous tussle with Rheingold through-out the final two furlongs of the 1972 Derby. It was a notable example of Piggott's supreme ability but, due to the circum-stances surrounding Williamson's late replacement, Roberto returned to virtual silence rather than the usual triumphant acclaim given to a winner of the world's greatest race. This post-race demonstration of support for the Australian broke out again, and in a more tangible form, following the very next event on the Epsom card for, as fate would have it, it was Williamson who rode the winner. 'Weary Willie' was accorded the cheers usually reserved for the Derby-winning jockey, but that was small consolation for losing by far his best opportunity to add his name to Epsom's roll of honour. For the remainder of his tragically short life Bill Williamson considered he had been done out of his rightful chance of Derby glory.

'Bill was certainly very upset' confirms Scobie. 'But we all have to live with that kind of thing in the racing world. Getting "jocked-off" as we call it happens to every rider sooner or later, and you could hardly blame Lester Piggott for taking the ride on

Roberto when it was offered. Of course, Lester is a great man for the telephone, always likely to ring up an owner or trainer and offer himself for a fancied ride. But that's all part of getting to the top, specially when you're riding as a freelance. But it was nice for Bill to win the Irish Derby on Steel Pulse just three weeks afterwards, beating Lester into third place on Ballymore and with Roberto trailing in two from last. I think he felt better after that.'

Williamson pulled off successive Arc de Triomphe wins on Vaguely Noble (1968) and Levmoss (1969). On the occasion of his second Longchamp big-race victory he edged out Piggott who was riding the brilliant mare Park Top. 'Most people thought Lester should have won that one, but Bill was at his best and "pinched" the race', Scobie says.

Bill Williamson quit the saddle at the conclusion of the 1973 season, for a short while preceding Scobie as manager of the Ravi Tikkoo horses. But he had never settled down fully away from Australia, and returned there in 1975 to become a starter. It was with great sadness that British racing supporters learned of this fine jockey's death following a short illness four years later.

Breasley also thought highly of Manny Mercer, elder brother of the highly-successful Joe who is, at the time of writing, in his 50th year, and is still riding winners galore. Manny was killed in a fall at Ascot in 1959 when still several months short of his 30th birthday. 'He was already a very good jockey and was potentially a great one. It was a tragedy', Scobie states.

16

The Winner that Never Was

Scobie Breasley's last winner as a jockey was the two-year-old Sentier in the Horris Hill Stakes at Newbury on Saturday 26 October 1968. Ironically, after 40 years devoted to the waiting game, he made every yard of the running on that momentous occasion. Not that Scobie or, indeed, the rest of us who were watching on that damp afternoon were aware that anything worthy of special recognition was taking place. The English Flat-racing season still had a full fortnight to go so Breasley was sure to ride a few more winners before his already-announced retirement from the saddle took effect. He had, for instance, a booking to partner the champion sprinter Be Friendly in the Vernons Cup at Haydock Park on the final programme of the term.

Be Friendly's owner, the distinguished racing journalist and commentator Peter O'Sullevan, was hoping that his fine horse would land the Vernons for the third year in succession and, at one and the same time, round off Scobie's legendary career on an appropriately high note. There seemed little reason to suppose that this carefully-laid plan was fallible. But the English weather, which should never be taken for granted, particularly during the second week of November, pre-ordained a dreadful anti-climax.

Haydock Park, a racecourse of considerable rural charm despite its location halfway along the East Lancs Road between the sprawling cities of Manchester and Liverpool, was prepared for a gala-day in its history. This track, the scene of Lester Piggott's very first victory, fully expected to pay right and proper respect to a great jockey of immense popularity.

In Manchester, oddly enough, the sun was shining. So it was on often-murky Merseyside. But Haydock Park was shrouded in a blanket of fog, cloying and immovable. Be Friendly was there, Scobie Breasley was there and so was his adoring public. The Haydock Stewards put back the advertised time of racing by half an hour and then another half an hour, hoping that the fog would lift. It didn't. Finally, racing was abandoned and Scobie's great farewell party was the flop of the season. Damp and disconsolate, Scobie had waited but with only the slightest shrug he turned back into the weighing-room to take off his racing silks for the very last time. Racegoers gave him a cheer anyway, sharing with the little Australian his disappointment. For the record, his last mount had been over the same course the previous day when he finished second on Arandora Star in the 12-furlong Salford Maiden Stakes. Arandora Star was beaten two and a half lengths by the favourite, Notonia, ridden by . . . yes, Lester Piggott.

So one of the greatest rivalries to quicken the pulse of British racing was maintained to the very end. How fortunate those who witnessed the 18-year battle between two of the world's greatest horsemen. And what changes took place on the Turf during its enactment. When Scobie arrived from Australia, slipping almost unnoticed into England, Lester Piggott was still claiming an apprentice allowance; such innovations as starting stalls and camera-patrol films were unknown. And so was betting tax! This was, in short, a period of change amounting almost to revolution within the racing world. But some values never alter and the conflict, even a stylized, within-the-rules conflict, in which two masters pit their skill, knowledge and experience against each other can be guaranteed to entertain, thrill and divide the watching public.

An entire dimension disappeared from the sport with Scobie Breasley's retirement as a jockey. Many racing fans hold the view that it has not, as yet, been fully replaced. Tributes to Scobie's career in the saddle fell thick on the ground. The Senior Steward of the Jockey Club was among those to praise him as were many fellow riders. But Breasley appreciated most of all the remarks of Sir Gordon Richards who said: 'I have never seen a greater jockey than Scobie Breasley. It has been a pleasure to be with a man who has been so great a credit to his profession'.

153

Lord Milford Haven with those dapper gentlemen of the Turf Scobie Breasley and Lester Piggott. Scobie had just retired from riding and offered his boots and saddle to benefit the Stable Lads' Welfare Trust. They made 750 guineas at the auction.

Only a year or two before his decision to stop riding, Scobie had been quoted as predicting that he would continue in the saddle until he was 60 years of age. At the same time he was busily dismissing any thoughts of training. So why this double change of heart? 'Really the two things went hand-in-hand', he points out. 'When I was keeping clear of injury and still riding well I did believe that I could carry on for a few more years. I loved riding and I loved the thrill of racing. And, of course, a jockey's income when he is at the top is considerable. Why give

154

up all that until you need to? But then came a few falls and old bones don't mend like young ones.

'A couple of years before I quit I was turning aside any thought of stopping but those knocks came hard and I decided that if I was going to give up I wanted to stay in racing and that meant training. And if I was going to train there was no point in delaying things much longer. It was a hard decision, perhaps the toughest I ever had to make in my professional life, but once I had made it, it was surprising how quickly I got used to the idea. After all, I'd had a longer run than most and won more than most. I told May that giving up riding would be like cutting off my right arm but once the moment came it wasn't nearly that bad.

'That's not to say it wasn't a wrench. Anybody who has been doing one job for 40 years and then takes on another is bound to feel uneasy for a while. But all the work involved in getting a training stable together helped to take my mind off the fact that I would not be riding the following season. Believe me, a trainer has so much paperwork and responsibility that there's very little time to think about anything else. Don't let anybody tell you that training racehorses is easier than riding. When you are a jockey and jump down after the race, that's the end. A trainer has a responsibility before the race, during it and after it. There are labour problems, gallops problems, jockey problems and management problems. You must keep owners happy and, most important of all, keep the horses happy. I thought I had a busy life as a jockey but I didn't know I was born!'

Breasley's enthusiasm for training, it would be fair to say, never quite matched his keenness for race-riding, but this by no means implies that he lacked either dedication or application in his new role. Scobie is not a half-hearted man. Whatever he does is undertaken thoroughly, as was his move into the late Walter Nightingall's stable at South Hatch on the edge of Epsom Downs ready for the start of a new challenge as the 1969 season loomed.

'South Hatch had a considerable training tradition and both May and I knew we had found the right place straight away. I did have an offer to train in France and considered it seriously, but our roots were pretty deep in England and in English racing by that time, so although both France and America were to figure in our future plans I was happy enough to start on home territory.

'Getting a stable of horses together is a complicated business. Quite honestly, I don't know how many young men can manage it these days. You certainly need a lot of capital and even if you have the cash it's important to get the right type of owners. It's not much use filling up the boxes with poor-quality horses not capable of winning decent races. Nor does it make sense to encourage owners who can't really afford the outlay to buy and keep their horses.

'Unpaid training bills have forced many men to the wall, so it is wise to know the pedigree of the owners as well as that of the horses they send you. I was lucky – or perhaps I was careful. My string numbered only 28 that first year, but about half of them came from Walter Nightingall's former patrons and Lady Beaverbrook, who had moved her horses to Gordon Richards when Walter died, returned a couple for me to train. I was also fortunate enough to get ten horses from Angus Kennedy who was to prove a real friend and a lucky owner. I also had horses owned by Sir Michael Sobell and his son-in-law Sir Arnold (now Lord) Weinstock, who became two of the most influential people in British racing. But at that time these big industrialists were comparative newcomers.'

Finding suitable staff can also be a major problem but in this respect, too, Scobie was fortunate. 'I had a good team at South Hatch and was very lucky to get Wally Mills as my head man. Wally had travelled horses for George Todd for many years and was a man of great knowledge and experience. No racing stable can be successful without a good head man and in Wally Mills I had one of the best.'

Scobie's training career was to be marked by a thoughtful approach. He was not a man to rush his fences and never over-raced the horses in his care. In effect, he brought to training the style he had so ably demonstrated as a rider – waiting his chance to strike to maximum advantage. That first season provided Scobie with just a dozen races worth £7,000 in

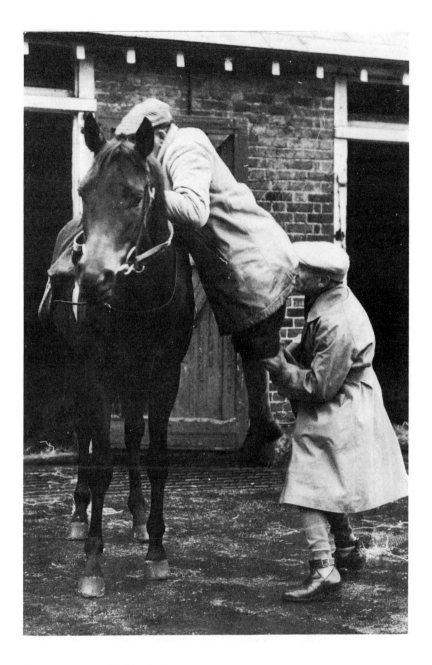

On you get . . . Scobie giving one of his lads the leg-up at South Hatch.

prize-money, a modest enough total, but a reasonable start for a new boy in the training ranks.

Meanwhile, Scobie was engaged on a programme of expansion, building 18 new boxes and a tack room to add to the existing accommodation at South Hatch. He also acquired an overspill yard nearby. His confidence was well-founded as during the 1970 season he saddled the winners of 23 races and increased his prize-money takings to more than £21,000. A readily discernible pattern was established by Scobie's training results over the years. 'I was not in the habit of setting myself target figures either in terms of winners or money, but most seasons we would produce about 20 wins to keep the ball rolling nicely', he says. 'And a few successes in valuable races helped put me on the map. The biggest one, of course, came with Steel Pulse in the '72 Sweeps Derby. That was a great day for all concerned.'

The Breasley training career lasted from 1969 to 1980. During that period he saddled 187 winners in Britain but the Curragh triumph of Steel Pulse stands out like a beacon. And not simply because it was a notable achievement for a Classic-winning jockey to train such an important victor, but also because it cemented Scobie's professional relationship with Ravi Tikkoo, an association which was to endure until the Australian's final retirement in 1983.

Ravi Tikkoo is a gifted and extraordinary man. Born in land-locked Kashmir, he became the owner of the world's biggest fleet of super-tankers, those mighty floating containers whose overall length is comparable to a skyscraper block laid on its side, the displacement of which is measured in hundreds of thousands of tons. Tikkoo hit British racing like a one-man Eastern tornado. He announced his intention of winning every major race on the international calendar within ten years. But great wealth and resources have never been a guarantee of success in the fickle world of the Turf, and the Tikkoo dream was never realised. But that has not prevented him from continuing to enjoy and patronize the sport and Scobie Breasley, naturally enough, regards him with both respect and affection. 'He was kindness itself to me and my family' Scobie says. I trained for him in England, France, America and then back in

England again. When I gave up training it was to become his racing manager. For nearly ten years Mr Tikkoo and I were a team and he treated me with courtesy and consideration, always making sure that we had the best of everything.'

Ravi Tikkoo selected Steel Pulse, a brown colt by the Washington International winner Diatome out of a Tudor Minstrel mare, on his own initiative and instructed the late Sam Armstrong to buy him, something the Newmarket trainer managed to do at a cost of only 4,000 guineas. Tikkoo's judgement proved sound as Steel Pulse developed into one of the best-staying two-year-olds of the 1971 season. Following minor wins at Brighton and Doncaster, he landed the seven-furlong Prix Georges de Kerhallet at Clairefontaine and the Grand Criterium de Maisons-Laffitte in which he beat Riverman and Mata Hari, winners respectively of the French 2,000 Guineas and 1,000 Guineas the following spring.

Allotted 9st 3lbs in the Free Handicap, he figured even higher in the French order of merit with 9st 5lbs. Only Hard to Beat, on whom Lester Piggott was to win the 1972 French Derby, was placed above Steel Pulse by the Société d'Encouragement handicapper. Steel Pulse ran fourth in the 2,000 Guineas at Newmarket, ridden by Jimmy Lindley and starting at odds of 6-1. He held every chance two furlongs out but the Rowley Mile course was too short for his stamina to take effect and he failed to quicken nearing the post.

Mr Tikkoo, who sometimes gives the impression that he is an impulsive owner and certainly an intuitive one, removed Steel Pulse from the St Gatien stable of Sam Armstrong soon after the season's first Classic. Armstrong was, to say the least, surprised when Scobie Breasley's horsebox showed up at Newmarket with the driver displaying a letter of authority ordering the colt's transfer.

But, almost needless to say, Scobie was delighted to have a horse of Steel Pulse's considerable proven ability and even greater potential in his care. He sent to France for Bill Pyers to ride the horse in the Derby at Epsom but Steel Pulse, although Scobie turned him out looking a picture, never reached the leaders and finished eighth. 'To tell the truth, I was a little bit

159

disappointed, as his two-year-old form had been so good', Scobie remarks. 'But there were some decent horses behind him and, in any case, I thought he might have just needed the outing and could have been upset by the change of stables. We decided to pull him out again for the Prince of Wales Stakes at Royal Ascot and that day Steel Pulse showed me what he could do. He was up against Brigadier Gerard, who was carrying all before him, so we were really throwing Steel Pulse in at the deep end. He ran great, and a furlong out looked as though he might test the great horse. In the end, we were beaten five lengths but this was a really good run and encouraged us to take Steel Pulse to Ireland.'

Eric Eldin, now a successful trainer, had ridden Steel Pulse at Ascot but Scobie relied on the big-occasion experience of his compatriot Bill Williamson for the Curragh Classic, worth a fraction under £59,000 to the winner that year. Fourteen runners went to post to race on what the Irish term yielding ground, an expression which translates to soft anywhere else. Four of the horses who had run against Steel Pulse at Epsom were in the line-up again: Roberto (1st), Scottish Rifle (6th), Manitoulin (11th) and Lyphard (15th). Also well-fancied was Ballymore who had won the Irish 2,000 Guineas for Paddy Prendergast when racing in public for the very first time but who had sidestepped Epsom.

Despite the strength of the opposition, the Tikkoo-Breasley party travelled to Ireland in high spirits, believing they had at least a sporting chance following the good Ascot showing of their runner. But Steel Pulse was weak in the betting market, freely offered at 10-1 while Roberto, partnered by Johnny Roe, Vincent O'Brien's retained Irish jockey, was a hot 15-8 favourite to complete the Derby double. Ballymore (Lester Piggott) started a 3-1 chance with Lyphard (Freddie Head) at 7-2. Lyphard, although behind Steel Pulse at Epsom, had been rated unlucky, Head being unable to keep him straight rounding Tattenham Corner and so giving away many lengths. The six-times French champion still seems to suffer steering problems at Epsom to the present day.

'Bill rode the perfect race' states Scobie. 'He had Steel Pulse nicely settled early on, moved him into fourth place on the turn

Roadwork at Epsom with Scobie leading the South Hatch team. Note these spanking new horse blankets.

for home and, to my eyes at least, always looked the winner from that point on. Mind you, Ron Hutchinson did his best to mess up the whole plan. He came flying through on Scottish Rifle to pinch the lead about a furlong and a half out. But Bill had it all in hand, drove Steel Pulse on just past the furlong marker and beat Ron by a length. It was an all-Australian finish with nothing else in sight.'

That was almost literally true since third-placed Ballymore trailed the first two by an official six lengths which actually

161

looked nearer ten from the Press stand. Lyphard, although not repeating his Epsom antics to the same extent now that he was fitted with blinkers, still disappointed. He was challenging at the distance but hung to the right under pressure and came home fifth. Roberto, possibly showing the signs of that desperately hard time in England, ran no race at all. Strongly ridden fully half a mile from the finish, he dropped right away to come home a sad and sorry 12th. 'Ravi Tikkoo was jubilant, I thought he might never come down', Scobie remembers. 'It was a very special moment for me, too, something for which I had been aiming during three hard-working years as a trainer.'

But what a demanding and temperamental mistress racing can be! Scobie's elation was never to be repeated, at least with Steel Pulse. In fact, Steel Pulse never again won a race of any description. His best post-Curragh effort was to finish fourth in the King George VI and Queen Elizabeth Stakes, won by Brigadier Gerard. From then on his form gradually deteriorated. The 1972 St Leger looked to be of dubious quality so it was perfectly reasonable that Steel Pulse should start favourite. But, having been off the racecourse for seven weeks, he may have lost the edge to his fitness. Alternatively, he may not have stayed Doncaster's extended mile and three quarter trip. Scobie remains uncertain.

Steel Pulse invariably did very well for himself at the manger and usually looked robust and barrel-chested. At Doncaster, however, he was positively portly. Scobie is well aware of that and says: 'It was difficult to be sure about his fitness. He was a good-looking colt, and powerful, but since he always carried a lot of condition I was left guessing sometimes. Working horses on the gallops is never quite the same as racing them and Steel Pulse may have fooled me before the Leger.' In any event, he finished last of the seven runners, the final Classic of 1972 going to Vincent O'Brien's Boucher (Piggott) who did not match up in terms of overall ability to the Steel Pulse who had carried off the Sweeps Derby.

There was nothing to lose by running Steel Pulse again so, although he had little chance of winning the Arc de Triomphe judging by his dismal showing at Doncaster, he was dispatched to Paris. But he sweated up and performed poorly, finishing well back behind the surprise winner, San San. Still he was not finished. Scobie tried him in blinkers for the Champion Stakes but, after running prominently for seven furlongs, he dropped out. His 10th and final race of 1972 was in the Washington International at Laurel. Perhaps surprisingly, Steel Pulse acquitted himself well by finishing third to Droll Role and Parnell and it was decided to keep him in training as a four-year-old. 'Unfortunately, he never really came to himself at four and ran only twice', says Scobie. 'It was a pity he could never match his Irish Derby form afterwards because he was a pretty good horse that day and I was very proud of him.'

Steel Pulse was bought by a syndicate of Australian breeders in 1973. They paid £370,000 for the son of Diatome who had cost Mr Tikkoo, you will recall, £365,800 less as a yearling. No wonder bloodstock dealing is such a popular method of gambling.

Overleaf: *The 1971 Cumberland Lodge Stakes at Ascot. Knockroe (Lester Piggott) proves too good for the Breasley-trained horse Great Wall, ridden by Jimmy Lindley.*

17

The Travelling Trainer

Lady Beaverbrook's Biskrah provided Scobie Breasley with another important 1972 victory by taking the two-and-a-quarter mile Doncaster Cup 48 hours before Steel Pulse's flop in the St Leger. In fact, Biskrah enjoyed a most profitable year. Prior to his good win in Yorkshire, the five-year-old had carried big weights successfully in the Goodwood Stakes, the Halifax Handicap at Ascot and the Guildford Handicap at Sandown Park, Geoff Lewis and Joe Mercer each winning two races on his back.

It was as recently as 1964 that Lady Beaverbrook started buying racehorses, seeking a pastime after the death of her husband, the Canadian-born newspaper magnate and statesman. Lord Beaverbrook himself had registered colours back in the 1920s but soon became disenchanted with ownership, although he continued to see the value of extensive coverage of the sport in his newspapers. His widow became a big spender in the bloodstock market, but although rewarded with many minor-league winners she tended to miss out on the really important prizes perhaps because of her addiction to the stock of that brilliant Derby and Arc winner Sea Bird II who, alas, did not seem able to bequeath his own ability to many of his off-spring. There were exceptions, notably Allez France, but Lady Beaverbrook was never lucky enough to buy one of these.

Biskrah's wins in staying races pinpointed Scobie's training versatility as the previous year his major success had come with the sprinter Royben, who achieved the rare distinction of landing both Doncaster's Portland Handicap and the Ayr Gold Cup, ridden on both occasions by Bill Williamson. Royben was owned by Angus Kennedy, one of Scobie's first patrons. Doncaster was to prove a happy hunting ground for Scobie during his training days as it was there in 1975 that Ravi Tikkoo's Hittite Glory first showed his potential by winning the Flying Childers Stakes, causing such a sensation in the process that when the grey Bruni put ten lengths between himself and the rest of the St Leger field later in the afternoon, racegoers were still discussing the extraordinary victory of the Breasley-trained two-year-old.

The 1975 Flying Childers really was a surprising race. Only five started, and of that quintet just two, Music Boy and Faliraki, seemed to hold a realistic chance. Consequently, the bookmakers offered 14-1 bar them and priced Hittite Glory at an amazing 100-1. 'They were silly odds and I was not really surprised when he won,' insists Scobie. 'I know he had finished a long way behind Music Boy in the Gimcrack Stakes at York the previous month, but he had won a decent Newmarket maiden in the summer and was badly hampered next time out in the Richmond Stakes at Goodwood. I certainly thought we had yet to see the best of him and fully expected him to run well up at Doncaster.'

Faliraki, winner of Royal Ascot's Norfolk Stakes for Curragh trainer Mick O'Toole, was beaten two furlongs out but Music Boy, odds-on, looked sure to win as Johnny Seagrave pushed him clear at that point. Hittite Glory had been towards the rear but little Frankie Durr started to make progress on him a furlong out, conjured up a devastating burst of speed in the final 50 yards and led a stride or two from the post to win by half a length. The bookies cheered, the vast majority of them having enjoyed a 'skinner' by not laying a single wager on the winner. But racegoers greeted this singular result in open-mouthed disbelief. No doubt many in the big St Leger day crowd regarded Hittite Glory's last-grasp victory as nothing more than a fluke.

Scobie knew otherwise. He was not a trainer to mistake his geese for swans but neither was he a man to harbour a champion unawares. Hittite Glory was, in his view, an exceptionally fast juvenile and well worthy of a tilt at the Group I William Hill

---

Overleaf: *Hittite Glory, nearest the camera, wins the 1975 Flying Childers Stakes at Doncaster. Scobie was not surprised at the success of his colt, ridden by Frankie Durr, despite the 100-1 starting price.*

Middle Park Stakes, which carried more than £22,000 in first prize-money, at Newmarket the following month. Hittite Glory completely validated Scobie's opinion of his ability in the big Newmarket test, but it was only in the very last stride that Durr got the colt's nose in front. 'I hurried down to ask Frankie if we had won but even he wasn't sure. It was a whisker but it was far enough', recalls Breasley with a smile of satisfaction.

Further drama was to follow with a Stewards' inquiry announced into what had undoubtedly been a very rough race. Hittite Glory, perhaps by Durr's design but more likely by accident, was the slowest of the eight runners to leave the stalls and found himself in last place with the remainder of the field tightly packed ahead of him. This was no worry for the first couple of furlongs but when the situation was unchanged only a furlong and a half from the finish Frankie Durr was clearly ill at ease and hoping that a gap would open up pretty damn quick. 'I'm sure Frank was worried because I certainly was' admits Scobie. 'But I was even more worried when just about half a gap came and Frank squeezed Hittite Glory through.' Royal Blue and Bruce Raymond appeared to get a bump at this point but just as Hittite Glory was making rapid headway on the inside he was much more seriously impeded by Duke Ellington, the eventual runner-up, hanging left and giving the Breasley colt a real knock. Only a tough customer would have shrugged off such a full-blooded clout but Hittite Glory did just that to grab the spoils by inches.

Stewards' inquiries are not open to either public or Press although the video-film recording may be viewed by media representatives once the verdict has been announced. However, it seems reasonable to conclude that the Newmarket officials acting that day decided that Hittite Glory was more sinned against than sinner. Anyway, he kept the race.

The immediate post-race clamour around the winners' enclosure is often turbulent on such occasions. Owners and trainers congratulate each other; the Press rush forward seeking future running plans and representatives of the major bookmaking companies are already offering ante-post prices on forthcoming events in which that day's principal horses are likely to run.

This is also the setting for post-mortems and, sometimes, rows and recriminations. In short, a bear-garden . . . and a fertile plot for the eavesdropper. One such reported – in print – conversations he claimed to have overheard between the then Senior Steward of the Jockey Club, Viscount Leverhulme, and Mrs May Breasley. It went something like this:

Lord Leverhulme: 'Many congratulations, I do hope Scobie had a decent bet on his winner.'
Mrs Breasley: 'I doubt it, my Lord. I don't think he's had a bet at all since he gave up riding.'

It should be pointed out, for the benefit of the unaware, that jockeys are strictly prohibited from betting by Jockey Club rules although, rather unfairly it might be thought, no such stricture applies to trainers some of whom are, in fact, among the heaviest betters in the business. Further, May Breasley says she has no recollection of the conversation with the Senior Steward taking place at all, but it is such a delightful story that it seems worthy of inclusion.

By the time of Hittite Glory's thrilling Middle Park win plans were already well advanced for the Breasleys to strike their tents again and move on. Ravi Tikkoo, by now much the most important client of Scobie's yard, had a fundamental objection to the imposition of Value Added Tax on bloodstock. His reasoning was perfectly valid since the Government of Great Britain was the only taxation authority among the major European nations charging VAT at the full rate on racehorses. France and Ireland, to give the prime examples, levied this tax only on the carcass value of horses just as they did with cattle, sheep or pigs. 'Mr Tikkoo was firm on his refusal to go on paying VAT – it was a matter of principle' says Scobie. 'And I agreed with him. British owners were being put at an unfair disadvantage.'

For a man of Ravi Tikkoo's resources, the answer was simplicity itself – move your trainer and his horses to France. Scobie was 62, hardly the time of life to set up home in a foreign land where the language itself would present a significant problem not only to the conduct of his work but in everyday living.

171

But he was not about to duck the challenge and at 4 am one frosty, foggy December morning he supervised the loading of 40 Tikkoo horses into transporters en route for their new quarters at Chantilly. 'It was sad – we didn't like leaving South Hatch and we didn't like leaving England. But it was exciting, too. I stood there rubbing my hands to keep warm and told the stable lads who were taking the horses "Off you go and learn your French".' As the last horse was being loaded he staged a defiant effort to stay, kicking at the door of his box. Ironically, that horse was named Return Ticket but he had to leave to catch the 8 am ferry from Dover with the rest.

Scobie's new quarters were palatial, 60 well-appointed boxes in a snug corner of the historic Chantilly-Lamorlaye training complex in the pine forests north of Paris. He had some pretty posh neighbours, too, with the headquarters of Baron Guy de Rothschild's racing empire just across the way. Chantilly is to the French Turf what Newmarket represents to its English counterparts, but while the little Suffolk market town is rather drab and surrounded by featureless Fenland, Chantilly is a gracious and beautiful place boasting an imposing château and set amid magnificent scenery. 'I'd ridden at Chantilly a few times and liked it – who wouldn't? – but learning a whole new routine in an unfamiliar country posed a few problems' Scobie admits. 'But the set-up there is wonderful with such a variety of gallops and walks through the forest. For my money, it is the greatest place in the world to train horses. I've never seen anything quite like it. Given time, we would have settled in quite happily but as things worked out we were to remain at Chantilly for only 11 months before hitting the trail again, this time for America.'

Scobie's short time in France was fruitful in terms of winners – 41 successes worth more than £300,000 – but the Classic hopes entertained for Hittite Glory failed to materialize. He finished last of the 11 starters for the 1976 French 2,000 Guineas having clearly failed to stay the Longchamp mile. Accepting this fact, his trainer at once redirected the son of Habitat to sprinting but his performances, with one notable exception, did not improve. Hittite Glory was again last in the July Cup at Newmarket and beat only one of 10 runners in the Prix de Seine-et-Oise. By far his best effort as a three-year-old came in the King's Stand Stakes at Royal Ascot in which he finished third behind the flying Yorkshire sprinter Lochnager and Realty, staying on in great style after being badly outpaced in the early stages of this hot five-furlong event which was run on fast going.

In the October it was announced that Hittite Glory had been syndicated at £4,000 per share to stand at the New England Stud in Newmarket. He may have been inconsistent but, on his day, was a very good horse indeed and a most attractive individual. Hittite Glory was soon producing winners and made the table of leading first-season sires in 1980.

The Chantilly sojourn came to a sudden, controversial and unhappy conclusion. The three-year-old colt Java Rajah, quite possibly the best horse in Scobie's Chantilly yard, was alleged to have shown traces of the stimulant caffeine in his system following a routine dope test. 'How the drug got there, if it was there at all, is a mystery', Scobie claims with conviction. Java Rajah had won a valuable handicap at Deauville on the Normandy coast in August and followed this up with another success at Longchamp, beating Kaole over 12 furlongs of the celebrated Paris track. It was that latter event which led to all the trouble and the eventual removal of the Ravi Tikkoo string from France. But before the verdict of the dope test was made public, Java Rajah demonstrated what a good and still-improving colt he was by running a most creditable eighth of 20 to Ivanjica in the 1976 Prix de l'Arc de Triomphe.

'It was a bombshell when I was contacted by the French racing authorities and was informed that my horse had given a positive test and that he stood to be disqualified from his Longchamp win, and that action might be taken against me as the trainer' Scobie says. 'The testing system in England is widely thought to be the best in the world but I had far less faith in the French. One thing I am quite positive about is that no caffeine or any other prohibited drug was given to Java Rajah deliberately by me or by any member of my staff.'

Ravi Tikkoo was furious and at once sprang to the defence of his trainer, publicly stating that in his view Scobie was being

Java Rajah, the horse whose disqualification led to Scobie's departure from France in 1976.

victimized by the Société d'Encouragement as a reprisal for a similar course of action taken by the Jockey Club in England againt Trepan, a colt trained at Chantilly by François Boutin. Trepan had been sent over to contest the Prince of Wales Stakes at Royal Ascot and won in spectacular style, beating Anne's Pretender by two and a half lengths after turning into the short Ascot straight back in sixth place. Rose Bowl, the odds-on favourite, could finish only fourth. Trepan's performance was a real eye-opener.

Three weeks later, he was back to give a repeat showing in the Coral Eclipse Stakes at Sandown Park, this time lowering the colours of the Guineas winner Wollow and more than confirming Ascot form with Anne's Pretender who this time finished 12 lengths adrift in fourth place. Boutin's stable jockey, Philippe Paquet, was the successful rider on both occasions. It is normal practice to perform a routine test on all Pattern race winners in England so, as a matter of course, Trepan gave a urine sample immediately following his brilliant victories at Ascot and Sandown. Both were found to be positive when analysed at the Equine Research Laboratory in Newmarket, probably the most advanced and sophisticated establishment of its kind in the world. Here we had the makings of a major international squabble between the two most powerful racing nations in Europe.

So it proved. Racing's entente cordiale has rarely come closer to falling apart in modern times. The French authorities, not to mention Turf followers on the other side of the Channel, were scandalized, outraged at the accusations being made against one of their most distinguished trainers. Nor was the situation helped by a positive rash of sensational disclosures in the British Press. A leading racing journalist reported François Mathet, the doyen of Chantilly horsemasters, as saying: 'Horses are being doped throughout Chantilly. I know what is being used and how it is being done'. No sooner were these words published than Mathet retracted them and claimed that his statement had been distorted. But the flames of controversy had already been fanned. Other stories followed and, as the Timeform's authoritative *Racehorses of 1976* pointed out, while they were seemingly based on nothing stronger than hearsay and rumour, they were doing considerable damage to the normally good relations of Anglo-French racing.

It was alleged that some French horses were being fed drugs to enhance their performances and also claimed that others were being given transfusions of their own blood before races in the belief that this practice, reputed to be used by some long-distance human athletes, provided extra pep. But the epidemic of stories about 'The Treatment', as it became known, were never more than so-called newspaper exclusives. No widespread malpractice was ever proved.

What was proved, at least to the satisfaction of the English Jockey Club's disciplinary committe, was that Trepan won at both Ascot and Sandown Park with prohibited substances

175

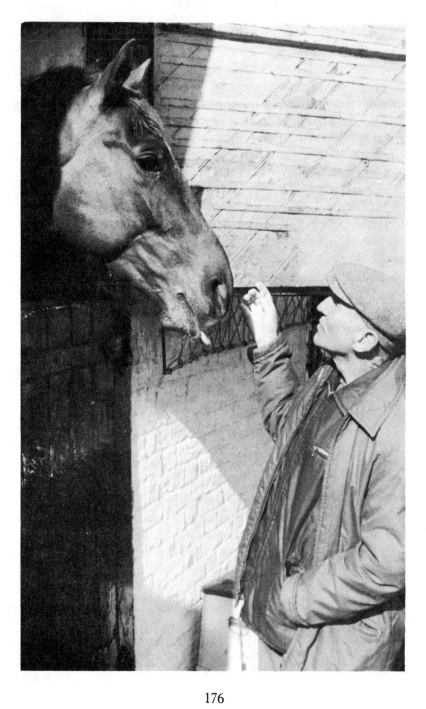

176

detectable in his bloodstream. The traces of caffeine and theobromine in the urine sample taken at Royal Ascot were attributed by Boutin to be a dose of the diuretic drug Hepatorenal which was mistakenly given to Trepan by a stable employee only 24 hours before the Prince of Wales Stakes. Boutin told the inquiry, held at the Jockey Club's London headquarters, that he gave some of his runners a diuretic when they were due to race but emphasized that this was normally discontinued at least three days beforehand.

The Stewards accepted François Boutin's explanation of the source of the illegal substances but still imposed the maximum fine of £500 for each breach of the regulations, also fining his employee £100. The sample taken from Trepan at Sandown was also said to contain traces of theobromine but the source of this was not established at the London hearing since Boutin stated that Trepan had received no medication during the two and a half weeks between his two races in England. The trainer was fined £250 in connection with the Sandown race and, of course, Trepan was disqualified in both instances meaning the loss of prize-money to his owner totalling almost £50,000.

The Jockey Club inquiry at which both cases were considered took place on 12 August. The following month – on 12 September to be precise – Java Rajah won the big Tierce handicap at Longchamp and was, apparently, positively tested for caffeine. A coincidence? All that was forthcoming from the Société d'Encouragement was a crumb dropped to English racing correspondent Jim Stanford, who was told by Société secretary Louis Romanet that the Java Rajah sample was similar in content to that shown by Trepan after the French colt had won at Ascot. Make of that what you will.

Ravi Tikkoo was, however, convinced that his horse and his trainer were being made scapegoats. And he was having none of that. Once again the millionaire oil tanker owner acted decisively, announcing his intention to withdraw completely from France and to take his string to the United States. This action was

Opposite: *Meeting a friend during evening stables at South Hatch – a vital part of every trainer's daily routine.*

Experts meet. Scobie talking with the late Fred Rimell, champion National Hunt trainer, while May listens in.

prompted not just because of the claims made against Java Rajah which Mr Tikkoo regarded as a completely unwarranted slur on the integrity of Scobie Breasley, but because the Société refused point-blank to make part of the urine sample available for independent analysis in England. 'You'd hardly believe what they told me' says Scobie. 'I still hardly believe it myself. "Oh, we're sorry Mr Breasley, there isn't any of the sample left" was the response to my request.'

Despite his protests and those of owner Tikkoo, Scobie Breasley was eventually told to pay a fine of 20,000 francs (£2,200) for his 'technical' offence and Java Rajah was disqualified. 'There was no way we were going to stay after that,' recalls Scobie, 'so the complicated process of moving lock, stock and horses across the Atlantic went ahead.'

18

A Question of Integrity

Absolute integrity is vital to the professional racing man or woman. Singular emphasis is placed on honesty in a sporting industry involving the transfer of huge sums of money by word of mouth alone. No jockey or trainer could possibly afford to be branded a cheat and allow such charges to go unanswered. How he might choose to refute them is a matter for the individual who believes himself wronged. Scobie's reply to the accusations of the French Turf establishment was, with Ravi Tikkoo's help and support, to simply shake the dust of Chantilly from his riding boots. Some 15 years earlier he had chosen a completely different course by suing two well-known racing journalists and their newspapers for libel.

Both the articles complained of were published in 1961 but, in the interminable nature of legal matters, it was not until November, 1963 that Breasley's action reached the vaulted halls of the High Court in London. He had become champion jockey for the fourth time just a week before. Scobie's suits were against Lt Col Tom Nickalls of the *Sporting Life*, the specialist newspaper which covers every aspect of both horse and greyhound racing, and Don Cox of the *Daily Herald*, a national newspaper which has since ceased to be published. Both cases were heard together as both journals were under the ownership of Odhams Press Ltd. The actions, heard by a jury of nine men and three women, before Mr Justice Havers, occupied three days. The judge celebrated his 74th birthday on the opening day of proceedings.

Lt Col Nickalls was sued over a comment under his by-line in the *Sporting Life* during October 1961. Scobie objected to the words contained in that article which read: 'Breasley never seems to shine on odds-on chances and here his horse failed by

179

one and a half lengths to reach Another Flash'. The race referred to was the Byfleet Stakes at Hurst Park in which Scobie was riding Operatic Society. Breasley's counsel, Mr Gerald Gardiner QC, told the court that the only reasons why a jockey did not shine on odds-on horses were either that he was incompetent or that he was pulling the horse. 'Both allegations are untrue in the case of Mr Breasley' counsel said. Up to that time, it was stated, Scobie Breasley had ridden 55 odds-on favourites and of that total only 19 had failed to win.

As a result of a letter from Mr Breasley's solicitors, said Gerald Gardiner, a paragraph had appeared in the *Sporting Life*, written by Lt Col Nickalls, stating that he owed an apology to Mr Breasley, who was a fine jockey and had won on 36 odds-on favourites during that season and lost on only 19. Mr Breasley had not accepted that the apology was sufficient recompense. It was ineffective. Scobie went into the witness-box to tell the jury of the importance he attached to preserving his good name in racing.

'It is very, very important and you would certainly not get any of the top-class riding jobs for a stable if you were under any suspicion at all. It is so important that it could decide whether you stay in racing or eventually get no rides and so have to drop out.' Sir Gordon Richards, for whose stable Scobie was then contract rider, was sitting in court to hear his jockey's obviously sincere words.

In the second action, Scobie claimed damages because of an article by Don Cox in the *Daily Herald* of November 1961. In that article, it was alleged, the newspaper reported events at the end of a race at Newbury and stated that a small group of racegoers bellowed insults at Breasley because he had failed to win the race in question. The article included the words: 'They accused Breasley of not trying after he was beaten on the odds-on favourite Indian Conquest and implied he had lost the race to benefit the bookmakers'. The article also said that certain punters called out: 'Is this another for the bookies? Is this another for Swift?'. It was explained by the *Daily Herald* that Scobie Breasley's daughter Loretta was married to the jockey Brian Swift, son of a West End bookmaker.

180

Scobie Breasley told the court that his daughter had married in October 1960 but added: 'I have had no financial dealings of any kind with Mr Swift senior or Mrs Swift'. Asked by his counsel if it was usual when a favourite had been beaten for disappointed punters to shout at the jockey, Scobie replied: 'No, but it does happen on odd occasions'. Nobody, he added, had ever suggested before that he had been paid by bookmakers.

Mr Gardiner was scathing in his remarks concerning the *Daily Herald*'s defence. 'Do they say that any national newspaper is entitled to report any piece of scandal or gossip it may hear and that it is all right for the paper to then broadcast it?' he asked. 'Mr Breasley is claiming that the articles have injured his reputation and the trust in which he is held by his profession – racehorse owners, trainers, fellow jockeys and the racing public.' The defendants denied that the words in either article were defamatory and said that they were published in good faith and without malice. They said they would rely on the full texts of the articles and not on the extracts of which complaints had been made.

Scobie Breasley, champion jockey of England, succeeded, at least in part, in putting right what he considered to be a gross unfairness. His action against Don Cox and the *Daily Herald* was upheld by the jury after they had spent an hour and three-quarters over their deliberations, but they did not find for him in the case involving Lt Col Nickalls and the *Sporting Life*. Scobie was awarded £250 libel damages in his litigation against Cox and the *Herald* but the whole exercise was financially costly to him. He had refused a sum of £500 paid into court by the *Herald* a month before the case, offered by way of settlement, and was ordered to pay all legal costs incurred by both sides since that date. Additionally, he was saddled with the full costs incurred on both sides for his unsuccessful action against Nickalls and the *Sporting Life*.

The two actions were estimated to have swallowed up more than £5,000 in legal and other fees or, perhaps more significantly, ten times the award made to Scobie by the High Court jury. Does he now consider bringing the actions to have been worthwhile? 'Yes, I think so', he says after due consideration. 'It cost me a lot of money but I think I made my point. You cannot afford to let people get away with damaging your reputation and while they may not have done so intentionally that was how I saw it. I have always tried to help newspaper reporters whenever I could because racing is very dependent on newspapers carrying news about the sport, but there must be a limit to what they are entitled to print. My whole object was to clear my name and I believe I did that. So it was money well spent in the long run.'

Perhaps this was a case in which all parties came out of court with something to celebrate. Tom Nickalls, who retired from the *Sporting Life* in 1968 but who is still active in racing journalism at the age of 80, commented at the time: 'I feel as happy as if I had napped a 100-1 outsider which won the November Handicap'. Don Cox, now manager of Doncaster Racecourse, was quoted as saying: 'I am delighted and feel the findings against me are solely because, in reporting remarks by a section of the crowd, I was guilty of a technical libel which only a lawyer could have foreseen'.

Scobie clearly does not subscribe to the much-quoted saying – perhaps invented by the newspaper industry – that there's no such thing as bad publicity. Neither Tom Nickalls nor Don Cox, both well-respected racing professionals, had any personal animosity against the jockey but Breasley's determination to proceed against them underlines just how strongly he felt – and still feels – when he gains the impression that he is under attack.

By and large, Scobie's relations with the Press have been amicable, if guarded, on his side. He numbers Peter O'Sullevan and John Hardie among his special friends from the British Press corps, and has always enjoyed a warm relationship with the distinguished Australian television and radio commentator Bill Collins, a cousin of May Breasley's. 'Bill has a long list of broadcasting credits and has covered racing, trotting and even an Olympic Games for the networks', Scobie says. 'He's a wonderful commentator and a real friend.'

But Scobie did once have a blazing row with a British newspaperman, Tim Fitzgeorge-Parker, formerly racing correspondent of the *Daily Mail*. This time Scobie went to war, not on his own behalf, but in support of his friend and fellow Australian jockey Garnie Bougoure. Scobie held the view that Fitzgeorge-Parker had been unfair to Bougoure in print several times, particularly when he had criticized him for dropping his whip when riding the good Irish colt Hardicanute. 'I thought this was wrong and silly' Scobie recalls. 'Every jockey – even the greatest of them – drops his whip sometimes. I've done it, Lester does it – we all do.

'So I went looking for Tim Fitzgeorge-Parker to put the record straight. Garnie was a good jockey and a particular pal of mine and I didn't want him to lose his retainer because of the things being written about him. But before I found my man another article appeared with some references to my old bones creaking in the wet weather. I wasn't too delighted about that, either. I bumped into Tim Fitzgeorge-Parker at Doncaster races one afternoon but when he saw me he started to walk away – the poor guy probably knew what was coming. In any case, I went after him and said something like "don't ignore me when I want to speak to you". I'm sorry to say I then called him a lot of names and told him he'd better watch out if we ever met in a dark lane. I said I didn't want to read any more of his comments about me, good or bad. It's a wonder he didn't chin me for what I was saying but I just saw red and it all came out. I'm glad to say Tim bore no malice and nor did I. Later in the year he came up to me at Longchamp one afternoon and we spoke together as though nothing had happened. That's the way rows should be settled.'

That all had been forgiven and forgotten of that clash between the jockey and the journalist became clear in 1980 when, in his biography of Sir Noel Murless, entitled *The Guv'nor*, Tim Fitzgeorge-Parker wrote these words in tribute to Scobie Breasley: 'Level-headed, businesslike, unemotional, a dedicated professional, Scobie was a superb judge of pace and excelled in split-second timing. He was a master at winning on two-year-olds or highly-strung fillies without giving them a hard race and, throughout his riding career, he gave racing connoisseurs continual pleasure'. Well, you can hardly say fairer than that, even if Scobie had not shown himself as level-headed and unemotional that day at Doncaster!

183

'The Press boys had this thing about calling me Grandfather Scobie after I won the Derby on Santa Claus and Charlottown' says Breasley. '"Listen to his old bones rattle", they used to write. I don't expect those sort of comments were intended to be hurtful in any way, it was just good newspaper copy no doubt. But nobody likes to pick up the paper every morning and be told how old they are. I got a bit fed up with it. After all, we all get older but when you're a jockey and still riding in big races it's not a very good idea for people to keep letting the whole world know you can hardly put one leg in front of the other!

'I'm sure I didn't ride too long. I knew when it was time to stop and one thing's for certain, the moment I made up my mind to give the game away nothing would have changed it. Of course, I told Sir Gordon first so that he could inform the owners and make plans for the next season. Then I announced it via the Press at Goodwood. May was with me and she was happy. She used to worry about me falling again which, I suppose, was understandable. So I simply gave notice that I was going to stop at the end of the 1968 season. Forty years is long enough. A few have gone on longer but not at the top. I wasn't going to have anyone doing the old boy a favour. When you're race-riding it's every man for himself. I never said "after you" to another jockey and I wouldn't have wanted or expected anyone else to pull over for me.'

But if Scobie's treatment by Fleet Street was not always entirely to the jockey's liking, he has many friends in Australia, England and beyond who are steadfast and loyal. Not by any means all of them came from within the racing industry, either.

Like most Australians, wherever they may be in the world, Scobie keeps an eye open for the cricket scoreboard and has two long-standing pals with famous names from within the ranks of that sport, Keith Miller, one of the greatest all-rounders to grace the game, and John Goddard, who captained that wonderful West Indies team of the 1950s which included Frank (later

Opposite: *'You need to lose some weight, Dad'. Loretta joking with Scobie and her mother during a family get-together in 1966. Scobie tipped the scales at about eight stones. He still does.*

185

Sir Frank) Worrell, Everton Weekes and Clyde Walcott, the fabulous Three W's of cricket's hall of fame. Mind you, both are keen racing fans, too. J. D. C. Goddard, as he appears in the cricket record books, has been a frequent guest of the Breasleys in England and often goes racing with Scobie. The roles tend to be reversed when Scobie and May are living at their home in Barbados for on the island, John Goddard figures among the leading racehorse owners. 'The Goddards are our neighbours in Barbados,' Scobie explains. 'We spend a great deal of time with them and they have come to England to visit us and their other friends here a lot. Lovely people.'

On their 1983 house call at South Hatch, John and Marcia Goddard were introduced by Scobie to Valerie Burholt, who has undertaken all the research and collation of material for this book. The co-authors are greatly in her debt for long hours of complex and dedicated work but, it must be said, Valerie is no cricket fan. Returning to the morning room some time later, she found John Goddard immersed in watching the current Test match on television. Ingenuously she inquired: 'Are you interested in cricket, Mr Goddard?'. To his eternal credit, and without even a smile, the famous West Indies captain replied: 'Yes, I am quite'. Mrs Burholt has, we understand, no plans to collaborate on the production of any cricket biographies in the near future.

Keith Miller's position in the annals of cricket is secure for all time and, interestingly enough, John Goddard takes the view that perhaps the only Test team of greater ability than his own West Indies side was the post-war Australian XI in which Miller was a star performer with both bat and ball. 'Keith and I have been pals for years and it would be hard to imagine anyone who is better fun', states Scobie. 'He's a great partygoer and it's always a laugh a minute when Keith is in the company. He likes a bet, too, and that's something he has in common with the majority of Australian cricketers. I think when Keith was playing he was sometimes more interested in which horse had won the

Opposite: *Supervising stable routine at South Hatch. Scobie holds the head of the lop-eared Portroy; jockey Tommy Carter is in the saddle.*

186

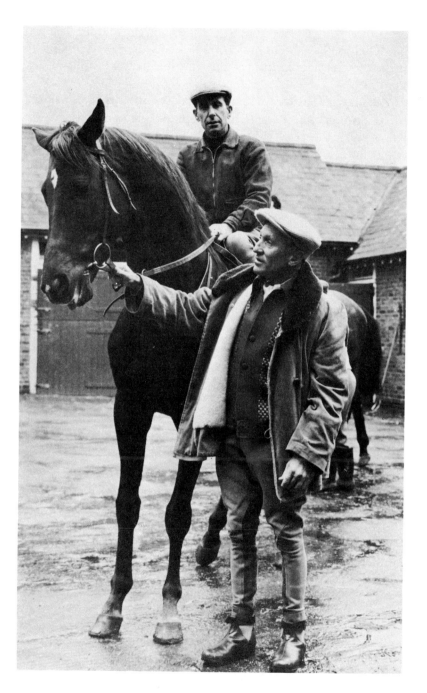

2.30 at Sandown than what was going on in the middle. I believe he developed a system of getting to know the racing results via his mates in the dressing-room even when he was batting in Test matches.

'The late Wally Grout, a fine wicket-keeper, was another who liked a punt, but on one tour to England he got into trouble and was owing the bookies rather too much. One or two of the Australian jockeys tried to put Wally right but, if you really need a winner that's the time you can't find one, so he was getting deeper and deeper in the mire as the tour came towards its close. Eventually, and just in time, Wally managed to find himself a winner at Newbury. I can't remember the name of the horse, or even the race, but it became known in the Australian dressing-room as "the Wally Grout Getting-Out Stakes".'

Scobie and May Breasley make a point of seeing Keith Miller whenever they are back home in Melbourne. 'It wouldn't seem like a proper holiday if we didn't have a party or two with Keith' Scobie says.

Opposite: *'Don't let them tell you that training is easy – the 'phone never stops and the paperwork keeps growing.'*

188

189

19

California Here I Come

Scobie Breasley's life-long policy of going anywhere in pursuit of winners, first illustrated by his momentous decision to quit Australian racing for Europe back in 1950, paid handsome dividends when he agreed to uproot yet again and cross the Atlantic to set up an American training operation in time for 1977. Training methods in Europe and the United States are as markedly different as the music of Beethoven and The Beach Boys. But Breasley's ability to adapt to changed circumstances had already been demonstrated quite clearly and even at the age of 63, a time of life at which the majority of men are content to walk the dog or potter in the garden, he met the new challenge head-on.

'You're never too old to learn a new trick or two and I went to America with an open mind to see if I could fit in and be successful', Scobie says. 'I need not have worried. We liked it there, enjoyed the life-style and, specially on the West Coast circuit, that lovely, sunny weather. California was quite like home for May and I and we had a lovely house at Arcadia, handy for the racing at Santa Anita and Hollywood Park. Once again, Ravi Tikkoo made certain that we had everything we needed. On the East Coast we lived very comfortably as well, based at Garden City, Long Island, for the racing at the New York tracks of Belmont Park and Aqueduct, Laurel and Pimlico in Maryland, Atlantic City and Monmouth Park, New Jersey. I used to have runners at Delaware as well.

'I'm not a great keeper of records, but we had plenty of winners both in the New York area and in California. In some ways training in America poses less problems than it does in either England or France. Things are more centralized with long periods of racing at a single course, and that cuts down all the travelling of which I was never very fond. American racing is well-organized and well-run. It may lack the charm and variety of the sport in England but everything possible is done to help the trainer and it's a pretty smooth operation. Training on the tracks and keeping your horses in the barns there makes you feel a certain lack of privacy but the system is suited to American-style racing and I had very few complaints. Certainly the prize-money is good.'

Scobie was fortunate to make a flying start to his American odyssey. His success was due largely to the efforts of Hunza Dancer, the colt who had run third to Grundy and Nobiliary in the 1975 Derby.

'I reckon Hunza Dancer liked America, too, and there was no holding him. He rattled off four straight wins including a fine stakes victory in the Bowling Green at Belmont and was just about the best grass horse in America that year.'

This winning sequence, which helped establish Scobie as a leading trainer in the USA, was in marked contrast to Hunza Dancer's efforts in England following his place in the Derby at odds of 50-1. Prior to Epsom he had won a minor 10-furlong race at Goodwood by four lengths with Lester Piggott in the saddle.

Although his pedigree was a polyglot from the stud books of several countries – his sire, Hawaii, was by the Italian stallion Utrillo II, who raced in both South Africa and the USA, while his dam, Oonagh, who was unraced, originated in Ireland – Hunza Dancer had actually been acquired by Mr Tikkoo in America. The colt cost Breasley's patron $80,000 at the Keeneland Sales in 1973.

British racegoers came to the conclusion that, as failure followed failure, Hunza Dancer was an ungenerous colt, belying his handsome head and sturdy frame. Timeform went so far to say, in *Racehorses of 1975*, that Hunza Dancer had become 'sulky and moody' and that when he felt disinclined to run there was nothing his jockey could do about it. A pretty damning indictment. 'It did look that way at the time,' Scobie admits. 'But he was a different horse when he got back to America and made a lot of people eat their words. Perhaps it was just the

191

Globe-trotting Scobie saddled plenty of winners during his two-year spell in America. Arjun, in the Ravi Tikkoo colours, scored at Monmouth Park, New Jersey.

Below: *Another winner for the Ravi Tikkoo-Scobie Breasley partnership. Grande Conde scored at Delaware Park during the summer of 1978.*

Another jockey in the family? Scobie's grandson Jason, splendidly mounted in the yard at South Hatch.

change of scenery which put him right, perhaps it was something else altogether, but whatever the reason he became a hell of a good horse in 1977.'

The Breasleys might well have settled permanently in the United States but for family ties back in England where Loretta, always the apple of Scobie's eye, and her children Kelly, Zonda and Jason were still living, Loretta's marriage to Brian Swift having been dissolved. Scobie hopes that his grandson will develop the talent to maintain the family tradition by becoming a jockey. Although barely into his teens, Jason already shows high promise and rides out for both his father and Geoff Lewis. 'He has very good hands and great all-round ability for his age. He's getting tall but is light and it would be wonderful if he could make the grade', Scobie says with pride.

When Scobie informed Ravi Tikkoo of his decision to terminate his stay in America and to pick up the thread of his life in England once again, Scobie's patron agreed and said that he would continue to keep horses with Breasley back at South Hatch in Epsom. 'That was a weight off my mind and cleared the way for us to make a fresh start without having to go looking for new owners and new horses.'

South Hatch had not been allowed to fall into disuse during Scobie's spells in Chantilly and America. He had leased the yard to a riding school on the understanding that the arrangement would be ended if he required the accommodation for training purposes again. 'Of course, it wasn't quite as simple as that. So until I could get back into the yard I was given special permission to keep some horses in the secure stables area at Epsom racecourse. I was most grateful to the management of United Racecourses for allowing this and to the Jockey Club who made a special exception to their Rules so that I was not left in the lurch.'

So Scobie Breasley rejoined the ranks of British trainers for the 1978 season, picking up just three minor races but happy to be back in the fold of his adopted country and once more in the swing of the English Turf.

By the following year, the South Hatch production line had returned to full-time operation and Scobie sent out the winners of 19 races to a total of more than £47,000. The itinerant Breasley was proving – if any further proof was necessary – that he could deliver the goods anywhere and at any time. His multi-national record was remarkable. In 1975 he had saddled 45 winners worth £69,000 in purses; in 1976 he was responsible for 40 winners in France, when only the larger and extremely powerful strings of Daniel Wildenstein, Jacques Wertheimer – the son of Rae Johnstone's old patron – and Nelson Bunker Hunt earned more money than Scobie generated for Ravi Tikkoo, and in 1977 Hunza Dancer alone had cleaned up nearly $200,000 for the Tikkoo-Breasley team in America.

Professional racing circles in England expressed some sur-

Opposite: *Scobie pictured shortly before his retirement from training, a lifetime's experience behind that gentle smile.*

prise, if general delight, both at Scobie's decision to return and at Mr Tikkoo's willingness to overcome his hatred of the British VAT system in order to continue his patronage. After all, this was a matter of principle and not of money. Had cash alone influenced him, the Tikkoo horses would not have departed for France at the conclusion of the 1975 Flat season, for that was a year in which Tikkoo had finished third in the list of leading owners in Great Britain.

Scobie had good cause to be grateful to Mr Tikkoo, therefore, and was pleased that the 1979 season turned out to be a rewarding one highlighted by the victory of Hanu in Ascot's Cornwallis Stakes. Hanu was by another good Tikkoo horse, Hot Spark, who, together with Steel Heart, had been taken away from Breasley and sent to be trained in Ireland by Dermot Weld when their owner was starting his long campaign against VAT on bloodstock in 1973. Light Link, Hanu's dam, also raced in the Tikkoo colours so there was no question of sales prices being inflated by the addition of VAT in the case of this horse. Hanu raced only four times as a two-year-old, winning his maiden at Lingfield Park as well as the Cornwallis and being in the frame after his other starts. He showed his best form over five furlongs during 1980, winning a mid-summer handicap at Goodwood and finishing runner-up to Valeriga in the Group III Premio Omenoni in Milan.

By this time, Scobie had reached the verge of retirement from training. It was his twelfth season in a craft which makes heavy and continual demands on time, skill and devotion to duty. Scobie Breasley, at 66, had earned at least semi-retirement from the everyday cares of the sport he loves. He had been professionally concerned with racing as rider and trainer for 52 years, a record in which he could take great pride.

There is an important point to be made about Scobie Breasley as a trainer. Because he had been so successful and so popular in his role as jockey, some people tended to understate his achievements once that aspect of his career had ended. However, had he never ridden or done so with less ability, it seems reasonable to assume that he would have been much more highly acclaimed for his training successes. In other words, Breasley the trainer suffered by comparison with Breasley the jockey. In fact, his training record indicates that he was a master of that craft as well. During those 12 seasons he saddled nearly 300 winners in a wide variety of places and under widely differing conditions. To average 25 winners or so a year from a string which rarely numbered more than 40 horses speaks volumes about both basic ability and consistency. With that modesty which is such a notable aspect of his personality, Scobie sums it up by saying: 'I did pretty well but I might have done better'.

So he might have, for example, if Great Wall, winner of the 1970 King Edward VII Stakes at Royal Ascot, was not unfortunate enough to have come up against the Triple Crown winner Nijinsky and the crack French colt Gyr in that year's Derby. Great Wall finished fourth but could easily have won in a less exalted season. The same might be said of Hunza Dancer five years later when that Breasley-trained colt met a well-above-average Derby winner in Grundy. But might-have-beens have never yet paid a bookmaker's bill or brought a letter of credit from the bank manager. 'You always need a bit of luck in racing' says Scobie, in philosophical vein. 'Looking back, I reckon to have had my fair share although I didn't always think so at the time. I suppose I might have trained two Derby winners if they had run in years when the competition was not so hot, but a lot of other trainers could say the same thing.'

Scobie Breasley, it can be stated without fear of contradiction, was a good trainer but because he was a great jockey the latter part of his long career in racing might always be seen as something of an anti-climax. From the end of the 1980 English Flat-racing season until 1983 Scobie acted as a conscientious racing manager to Ravi Tikkoo, offering his expert knowledge to that owner's current generation of trainers and perfectly content to take a less public role. 'It kept me in touch and gave me an excuse to go off racing when May might have had some ideas about going shopping for a new dress' he says with a smile.

In Conclusion

Few professional sportsmen in a worldwide context have lived a fuller or more satisfactory life than Scobie Breasley. That his rewards, both financial and personal, have been achieved through his own remarkable skills and their careful application, is unarguable. It is a very long way from the sleepy streets of Wagga Wagga as that town reposed in the early years of the century to the great racecourses of Europe and America, both in terms of miles and time. But Scobie bridged vast distances and several decades with apparent ease, always able to rely absolutely on the natural talent he refined until it was matched by very few of his contemporaries.

That he could remain agreeable, entertaining and a loving family man during that process suggests that he is also, and perhaps most importantly, down-to-earth and uncomplicated. For 48 years he has received the support and encouragement of his wife May. 'Scobie and I have something worthwhile' she says with obvious affection.

It is difficult to place Scobie Breasley's career in the general pattern of international racing for the very sound reason that he is a unique figure. But there can be little doubt that he was one of the finest riders of his time and, quite possibly, throughout the history of his sport. Just to watch Scobie come from out of the blue with one of his perfectly-timed late runs was among the Turf's most compelling sights. The hardest-pulling, least-manageable of horses went sweetly for him, responding to the silken touch of a master. Scobie Breasley won races by finesse rather than force.

No-one who watched him ride is ever likely to forget. The far smaller number of people to gain first his confidence and then his friendship consider themselves privileged.

A moment to reflect. Scobie in his office at South Hatch surrounded by pictures of family and friends.

The last word must be his own. 'Racing gave me a wonderful life. I'd like to think I gave at least a little bit back. Given it all again, I don't suppose I would make a lot of changes.'

THE JOCKEY CLUB
(Incorporated by Royal Charter in 1970)

Telegraphic Address
Joclub
London Telex
Telex 21393

Registry Office, 42 Portman Square, London W1H 0EN / Telephone: 01-486 4921

November 25, 1980

Dear Scobie

I understand from the Licensing Committee that you
have formally relinquished your trainer's licence, although
we had of course read the news of your impending retirement
in the Sporting Press.

I felt I could not let the occasion pass without writing
to you on behalf of the Stewards of the Jockey Club at the
close of such a memorable career as both a jockey and a trainer.

I think I am right in saying that you continued to ride
regularly up to the age of 54, but I am not sure for how many
years you rode in England after your arrival from Australia.
The age at which you continued to ride in the top flight
must be quite exceptional and, indeed, your career as a
jockey must be considered as one of the finest ever.

On a more personal note, I am sure one of the more
pleasing periods of your long career must have been the many
years with Gordon Richards at Beckhampton, and my own family
of course have always been very grateful for the many good
winners you rode for my Father at that time.

May I take this opportunity of thanking you for the
great contribution you have personally made to world racing,
and particularly in this country. I and the other Stewards
of the Jockey Club would like to wish you success and happiness
in your new role.

Yours sincerely,

Senior Steward

200

Index

205